Mark Martin

DRIVEN TO RACE

Mark Martin

DRIVEN TO RACE

By Bob Zeller

Foreword by Mark Martin

Design by Tom Morgan

David Bull Publishing

Library of Congress Cataloging-in-Publication Data
Zeller, Bob, 1952-
    Mark Martin : driven to race / by Bob Zeller ; foreword by Mark Martin.
        p. cm.
    ISBN 0-9649722-3-9 (alk. paper)
    1. Martin, Mark, 1959- . 2. Automobile racing drivers--United
States--Biography. 3. Stock car racing--United States. I. Title.
    GV1032.m36Z45 1997
    796.72'092--dc21
    [B]   97-3191
                                                       CIP

Printed in Hong Kong
Book and cover design: Tom Morgan, Blue Design

10 9 8 7 6 5 4

David Bull Publishing
4250 E. Camelback Road
Suite K.150
Phoenix, AZ 85018
602-852-9500

Photo credits

Rich Chenet: 6. **David Chobat**: 2, 3, 8, 106 (bottom), 108, 111, 114 (bottom), 119, 120, 126 (middle and bottom), 127 (bottom), 128, 129, 131, 133, 139, 140, 141, 143 (top and bottom), 149, 153, 154 (bottom). **Brian Cleary**: 115 (top), 130, 135, 136, 145. **Tom Copeland**: 142, 150/151, 152 (bottom), 158. **Bryan Hallman**: 132, 137, 138, 152 (top). **Kenny Kane**: 121, 146, 147, 155, 156. **Don Kelly**: 150, 151, 154 (top). **Larry McTighe**: 160. **Sam Sharpe**: Cover, 1, 148, 159. **T. Taylor Warren** 112, 114 (top), 116. All other photographs and materials are from the collections of Mark Martin, Julian Martin, Jackie Martin, and Larry Shaw

Photo captions:

Page 2: Mark and Terry Labonte chatted about racing technique before the driver introductions for the 1996 Busch Clash in February at Daytona.

Opposite: Now in his second year of racing, Mark still has a cherubic look on his face. But at 16, he could race with the roughest competitor at any local track.

Page 6: At speed at Phoenix, 1995.

Acknowledgments

Without the stories and photographs contributed by the Martins—Mark, Julian, Jackie, and Arlene, as well as by Larry Shaw—this book would not have been possible. They were generous with their time and, in their interviews, unhesitating and frank. Although they could have placed restrictions on what we included in the book, they did not. During the first eleven years of Mark's career, Jackie assembled one or two scrapbooks for every season. This invaluable resource provided the framework for the book, and was handsomely complemented by Julian's photographic memory and his endless supply of stories. In addition, Julian and Shelly Martin were gracious hosts during our visits to Arkansas. Thanks to the editors at Landmark Newspapers, and to Ann, Sara and Jesse Zeller, for their patience with this project. Thanks also to Jack Roush, Steve Hmiel, Robin Pemberton, Bill and Gail Davis, Wayne Brooks, Banjo Grimm, Ed Howe, Ray Dillon, Rusty Wallace, Dick Trickle, and Larry Phillips.

Benny Ertel saw the possibilities for Mark's story and was enormously helpful in coordinating the project. Lori Halbeisen and her predecessor, Diane Hollingsworth, at Roush Racing were a ready resource at the tracks and provided Mark's statistical information. Photographers Rich Chenet, David Chobat, Brian Cleary, Tom Copeland, Bryan Hallman, Kenny Kane, Don Kelly, Larry McTighe, Sam Sharpe, and T. Taylor Warren searched through their archives to provide the later photographs that are not from the Martin and Shaw collections. Special thanks to Steve Spence at *Car and Driver* and to Jean Cummings for the careful read they gave the manuscript. Their suggestions have made the book stronger.

Bob Zeller
David Bull

Foreword

There's very little thrill and excitement in what we do today compared to the early days.

Back when I started racing in 1974 we never expected to do as well as we did. We didn't know we were going to be any good at it. We were always surprising ourselves. I was only fifteen and my father and I had decided to go racing. It was all brand new to us.

I wanted to do this book so fans who didn't know me or know where I came from could find out what got me to NASCAR racing and where I am today. This is the story of how I got to be who I am. Your background, your experience is *you*. That's what makes you who you are. The way you were raised, your life, your experience—that's what makes up every individual.

When I look back at it, my background growing up in Batesville was unbelievable. I won't ruin the stories by going into detail here, but when I was a boy, Batesville was like the Wild West, with very little law around. My parents—especially my dad—were hard-working and hard-playing, often to extremes. Growing up, we had a tremendous work ethic. That and the drive and determination I got from my mother and my father have had a lot to do with my being successful.

When I started racing in the American Speed Association short-track stock car series, I won Rookie of the Year my first year. The next year—1978—I went on to become the youngest champion in ASA history and won a total of four championships. But my goal was always to go Winston Cup racing, and in 1981 I ran my own cars on a limited schedule. Since 1989 I have been the only driver to consistently finish in the top six in points every year. I am lucky to be doing exactly what I've always wanted to do. I am living my dream.

Bob Zeller, the author, did an awesome job of capturing the stories and excitement of the early years racing with my dad. Most people don't know about those stories—even my wife, Arlene, learned some things that made her laugh. Not a lot of people know about my early NASCAR career, either, so this book will give you a good idea of the setbacks I had to overcome and the amount of focus and determination it took to get where I am today. Maybe you'll see a bit of your own experience as you learn more about mine.

Thanks for reading my story.

Mark Martin
Daytona, February 1997

Left: At Pocono, Mark signs autographs for the many fans along Autograph Alley.

Right: At the end of the 1974 season, Mark won his first-ever race on asphalt at the new five-eighths-mile Stuttgart Speedway in Arkansas.

"I'm the fastest seven-year-old they got!"

Above: Mark's first-grade portrait. He was six years old. **Left:** Mark took it as a personal challenge to rack up as many miles on his bicycle's odometer as he possibly could. Julian says, "Mark went through a pickup truck load of tires. He tried to average ten miles a day and five of them must have been sliding."

On a hot July afternoon in 1974, somewhere in west Texas, Julian Martin slipped out of the passenger seat of the huge eighteen-wheeled truck, took a final look toward the horizon and crawled into the sleeper compartment behind the cab. As he closed the curtains and settled in for a nap, he knew the big rig was in capable hands. His fifteen-year-old son, Mark, was behind the wheel.

Mark wasn't even in tenth grade yet. He was barely five feet tall and just over a hundred pounds. He needed a couple of cushions for a booster seat. But he was good behind the wheel. Julian had been teaching him how to drive since the boy was five. Mark could drive anything—bicycles, motorcycles, cars, trucks. He had even begun driving race cars. He was a quick learner. And he was a confident driver, even though he had to spread-eagle his arms to grip the truck's big steering wheel.

Even at fifteen, Julian believed Mark was already a better driver than he was in some respects, and that made him happy because Julian considered himself the fastest and most fearless driver in his hometown of Batesville,

Using his $1,000 savings, Mark assumed the lease of this 1973 Kenworth when he was twelve. A local trucker was unnerved by the fuel crisis and wanted out of the business. Mark then leased the truck to Julian's company.

Arkansas. But as Julian drifted to sleep, he knew his son had a lot to learn. At that moment, he was too young to get a driver's license.

By 1974, the Julian Martin Trucking Company had a fleet of more than thirty-five refrigerated trucks. He was one of the most successful men in Batesville. And once a year, at the height of the California produce season, when every truck was rolling, Julian and Mark would make the trip west together.

Suddenly, Julian awoke to the shouts of his son. Then Mark was slapping the plastic curtain that separated them.

"Dad, get up here!" he shouted.

"What's the matter?" a startled Julian yelled back, scrambling out of the sleeper.

"You gotta take this thing over," Mark said. "One of your trucks just passed me. Your truck can't pass my truck. *I won't have that!* Get up here and make this truck outrun him!"

Julian was relieved, and amused. "Well, okay," he said. Apparently, Mark had gotten himself in a

For years, Mark and Julian spent every Christmas from morning to nightfall washing and photographing the trucks at a nearby factory. Christmas was the only day all the trucks were in the same place at the same time.

race with one of Julian's wildest drivers. Julian was quick to the challenge.

"Now don't let off," Julian ordered. said. "Hold it on the floor! Don't even crack it. Slide up in the seat."

Mark held the accelerator to the floor as Julian slipped behind him and slid his foot down Mark's leg. At more than seventy miles per hour, they completed the tricky switch and Mark moved to the passenger seat.

This was Mark's personal truck. It ran with his father's fleet. But Mark owned it, helped maintain it and was proud of it. He'd usually wash it himself at the fleet garage in Batesville. And he insisted that his father keep it tuned so it would outrun all of the other trucks on the lot.

And now, as the speedometer topped eighty miles per hour, Julian was driving the truck to its limit. The oil temperature was going up. The oil pressure was going down. The engine was screaming. But Julian passed his own truck. They were both happy about that. Julian kept the hammer down, rolling flat-out across the open, barren land that stretched out in front of them.

To Mark Martin, his father was the greatest man in the world. Julian Martin was reckless, wild and crazy, but he was also generous and loving.

"You couldn't love a son more than he loved me," Mark says today. "There was never any question about that, even with all the things that we went through and all the mistakes he made. He's an unbelievably generous person, not only with his son, but with everybody.

"I hated this damn truck," Julian says. "There were a lot of feed trucks hauling out of Batesville in 1959. We raced all the time. This son of a bitch was slower than smoke off a turd. I found that I could start it, then loosen the distributor and set the time way up, and that this would help me outrun the Chevies. But if I ever killed the engine when it was hot it wouldn't restart. I would set Mark in the seat beside me when he was a baby. His very first sentence was 'Son of a bitch won't start!'"

"He is strong. And he is tough. Crazy and tough. I saw a lot of people fight in my childhood. But I never saw one man stand up to him. He was too crazy. I never saw my dad have to whip any-body—*ever*. When he is mad, you don't mess with him. And he is fun. He's done a lot of crazy things, but usually they were fun."

Julian Martin was born in Batesville on January 5, 1936. He grew up in the tiny, roughhewn, rural village of Concord, eighteen miles southwest of Batesville. And his own father, Clyde, taught him to drive as Julian taught Mark.

"When I was ten years old, I was driving a truck," Julian recalls. "When I was thirteen, I was going back and forth to Little Rock, hauling feed."

Christmas in the mid-sixties. Mark and Julian strike a pose for Jackie. Mark is four or five years old.

He crashed for the first time when he was eleven while driving his cousin around. "I tried to leave the country," he says. "There were some bluffs a mile or two through the woods. I headed for the bluffs. I fig-ured I would probably have to live there for the rest of my life. But my uncle lived up the road. He heard the wreck and caught me. I didn't get yelled at much. They were glad we were okay."

It was the first of many crashes. Julian's worst, a motorcycle accident in August, 1971, left him per-manently disabled, although one can hardly tell upon seeing him. His mangled right hand is missing parts of two fingers. He lost his right kneecap and his right ankle is permanently fused.

"I was extremely wild and reckless and I didn't ever feel like rules were made to be followed," Julian says. "I think a thrill is worth just about any risk and the bigger the risk, the bigger the thrill. I used to be scared that God was going to make me a preacher because he saved me so many times."

Julian went to work for his father, who owned a feed business and raised chickens and turkeys. Julian was always a hard worker. But it was tough to get ahead in the hill country of Arkansas.

In 1957, Julian married Jackie Estes, who was also from Concord. She was one of the prettiest women in the region, and matched Julian step for step in his appetite for fun and high-speed adven-ture. She had a five-year-old daughter, Glenda, by a previous marriage, whom Julian adopted. Mark was born January 9, 1959, just four days after Julian's twenty-third birthday.

"By 1959, I was married and had two kids and I was making fifty bucks a week working six days,"

The first truck that Julian bought new was this 1963 International with a trailer equipped with a Briggs and Stratton-powered cooler. The school bus in the background (right) served as the company's office and tool room.

Jackie helped make Julian's fledgling trucking company a success by managing the bookkeeping while Julian ran the operations.

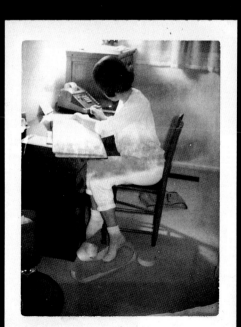

At fourteen, Glenda Martin beat a grown man in a drag race Julian instigated. She later won a trophy at the Newport Drag Strip driving Julian's pickup. Her high school graduation present was a 1970 Chevelle 396 that she kept spotless and used to beat the

Julian says. "So I bought this Ford bobtail truck and started hauling eggs to Memphis and St. Louis. Then I added a truck a year for the next three or four years."

In 1964, he moved to Batesville and continued to build his trucking company. His first eighteen-wheeler was a refrigerated 1963 International. The refrigeration unit, located in the nose of the trailer, consisted of a lawnmower engine, a block of ice and a squirrel-cage fan to blow cold air through a simple duct system. His office, shop, and parts room was a 1950 Ford school bus with all the seats removed. He parked it permanently in a vacant lot he rented for ten dollars a month at the corner of Fourteenth Street and Chaney Road in Batesville. Julian had the phone company install a pay phone over one of the rear wheel wells. He sat on the hump of the wheel well, gradually building a trucking business. In the summers, the sweat would pour off his brow as he talked business on the phone.

"It was hard. It was difficult," his ex-wife, Jackie, remembers. "We just had this spot of ground and this old, abandoned school bus. And when the drivers came in, they all just worked out on the ground. But we felt sure we were going to make it."

Mark, an only son, grew up around his father's trucking business. But as a youngster, he had other passions besides motor vehicles. He played Little League baseball. And on the ballfield, his greatest talent was speed.

During the year he played Little League, Mark (lower left) would often leave notes for Julian at the office signed "The Great Base Stealer." Mark prided himself on being the team's fastest runner.

This cowboy suit was a present on Mark's fifth birthday. He was showing Julian and Jackie what a quick draw he was with the six-shooters. "Unlike now, he really liked to pose for pictures back then," Julian says.

Julian remembers: "One day when he came back from practice, he said, 'I'm the fastest seven-year-old they got.' He wasn't a great batter or anything. His specialty was stealing bases. He'd come by my office when I wasn't there and leave a sheet of paper on my desk and sign it, *The Great Base Stealer*."

The young driver and ballplayer also was a ceramic potter. Today, when Mark visits relatives in Arkansas, he will notice an urn on a shelf, or a drinking mug on a mantel, and recognize it as his own work.

"I made all kinds of stuff," Mark remembers. "I gave all my relatives Christmas presents. I probably made 100 pieces. I wound up with my own kiln. I still see the stuff. But I don't have any of it. I'm not into keepsakes."

Another hobby was tropical fish. He started with a small bowl and some guppies. Before his interest waned, he had moved to a forty-gallon tank and was skillful enough to recognize and treat tropical fish diseases.

Mark's first wheels were bicycle wheels.

"I got a speedometer, and one of my goals every day after school was to put ten miles on it," he says. "I wanted to see those miles be big. I wanted to see 100 and some miles. I wanted to see 200 and some miles. I don't remember how many miles I ever got on it, but I wore bikes out. Most people make bikes last forever. I wore bikes out."

Mark remembers that he began asking for a mini-bike when he was about eight years old. "I wanted a go-cart," he says. "But my mom and dad wouldn't hear of that. They said you can run under cars. It took me longer than I thought it should to get a mini-bike. I even had a friend who had one for awhile before I got mine. I finally got mine, and I wore it out. It drove my father crazy keeping it up."

"That son of a bitch stayed broken all of the time," remembers Julian. "He brought it to the trucking place one day and I worked on it and finally got it fixed. At that time I had ten trucks. And I told him, 'I don't know which would be worse, trying to run ten trucks or trying to run ten damn mini-bikes.' "

"Well, about fifteen minutes later, the phone rings. I picked it up. And Mark didn't say hello or anything. He said, 'It would be ten mini-bikes.' "

"Because that thing had already broken down again."

Although Mark's parents made him wait to get a mini-bike, Julian started giving him driving lessons when he was five years old.

"I did him just like my daddy did me," recalls Julian. "I gave him a lot of room. I let him do things, sometimes when he was too young. And fortunately he didn't kill himself and didn't tear too much up. He handled it real well. If you give a kid a lot of rope, and they don't kill themselves, that works real good."

Julian started by making Mark stand in his lap and take the wheel of the car. It was always a fast car, of course, and as Mark steered, Julian would go faster, sometimes reaching seventy-five to eighty miles per hour.

"And as he learned, I put more speed into it," Julian says. "The bigger he got, the faster I'd take him through the turns. A lot of times, we were on these country gravel roads. There was never any traffic and it's real easy to slide.

"So I'd take him through turns where he didn't have any choice. He was going to slide or he was going to wreck. He'd have to counter-steer. A lot of times, he'd beg for mercy. He'd want me to slow down. And I'd laugh and Glenda would laugh. She would come along. Glenda had already been through the treatment when she was younger. I'd have her running through ditches and damn near into fences just beggin' me to take the wheel. And I wouldn't do it.

"So we'd tell Mark, 'You can do it! You gotta do it or we're going to wreck!' And it scared him. But it was also fun. And I don't remember me ever having to rescue him."

"What he did would scare anybody," says Mark. "But he wouldn't take the wheel. He just wouldn't let me quit. I grew up driving, from

Left: Posing on one of the family's cars around 1970, Jackie looked more like a model from the New York Auto Show than a housewife from Batesville, Arkansas.

Though they worked tremendously hard, the Martins had fun as a family, occasionally going for boat rides on Greer's Ferry Lake in Heber Springs, Arkansas. Mark is at the helm in this mid-sixties photograph.

standing in my dad's lap in a car, to sitting in his lap driving a truck, to him sitting on the doghouse of the truck and me driving, to eventually me driving it solo. My dad always put me in control of things way beyond my age. He always grew me up real fast. But in a lot of ways, he was just a big kid having fun. And we did have a lot of fun."

Julian's sense of fun was sometimes extreme. Once, when Mark was seven and Glenda was fourteen, Julian decided to challenge a local fellow who owned a hot car. There was a long stretch of straight, flat road just west of Batesville at the foot of Brock Mountain where Julian and his friends drag-raced.

"I went into this old country church one Wednesday night and called this guy out of church. The double doors were open, and I just slipped in and motioned with my finger for him to come with me. So he came out and we went down and raced.

"We made our bets and then I let him beat me a couple of times. And then I told him, 'You think that's something? I've got a fourteen-year-old daughter at home who can kick your ass.'"

The wager grew considerably. Then Julian went home and brought his daughter out. Glenda won going away. And in the moments before the race started, seven-year-old Mark scampered behind his father's car and coated the rear tires with Purex to soften the rubber for better grip.

"When Mark was ten, he and I built a fun car for ourselves to play with," Julian says. "He had kinda long hair then, just a little bitty chubby kid with long hair, and I would load my buddies up and say, 'Let's have ol' Mark take us for a ride.' We'd get in the back seat, because it was more fun to watch it from there. I had taught him, 'When you shift gears, you get it in gear or you break the damn stick off. Don't ever let me hear you get it part way in.' So this ten-year-old kid would get behind the wheel, and he'd take off and *slam* through the gears. And every time he'd shift, his long hair would jump off the back of his head."

There was a method to Julian's madness. Several of his friends had been killed in high-speed crashes on the twisting, two-lane roads around Batesville.

"I encouraged Mark to learn to do what I was doing because I felt like the parents of some of my friends who had gotten killed had sheltered them too long. And when they finally turned them loose, they went too crazy too quick. And I didn't want that to happen to my kids," Julian says.

"It was really a lot of fun to have a son come along and to progress into being able to do what you like to do, and do it real well. And enjoy it, too. That made me extremely happy. And I could see a potential of him being better than I was."

Christmas Day in the late sixties. Julian takes a break from assembling the toy truck on his lap to snack with Jackie. Mark looks up from the lower left.

[20]

And so Julian kept pushing his son. He was demanding, and at times he pushed too hard.

When Mark was twelve, he and his father took a truck trip in a long-nosed Peterbilt with a thirteen-speed transmission. They'd been in Ohio, and they were back in Arkansas, taking a shortcut through the hills on a narrow, winding two-lane road. Mark was behind the wheel.

"A thirteen-speed transmission is fairly complex for a twelve-year-old," Julian says. "The whole truck is fairly complex for a twelve-year-old. But he was driving it smooth, and he was shifting gears without the clutch, which is the best way if you're good enough. He'd just float it in and out of gear."

"But when you hit a real steep hill with a loaded truck like that, you can downshift a lot faster if you'll tap the clutch just to get it out of gear, and bring the RPM up and drop it in the next lower gear. Well, he's doing it real smooth, but I'm trying to tell him if he did it my way, he could go faster. And I was riding him to do it."

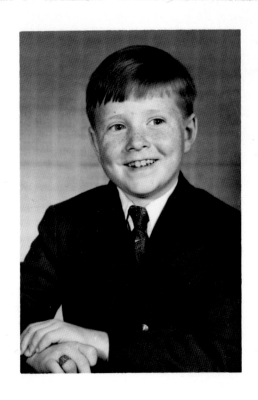

Mark's formal portrait was taken in 1967 wearing his new Easter suit. He is eight.

They went through a tiny town with a couple of street lights. Just as Julian glanced at his son, the light crossed Mark's face. Julian saw tears running down his cheeks.

"That made me feel pretty bad," Julian recalls. "And he and Glenda told me later that they felt like they could never please me. I'd always point out their faults. But he was damn near perfect at age twelve driving that truck. And the only thing I could find wrong was what I was telling him. But to him, I was disapproving."

As wild and free-spirited as his parents were, Mark was the opposite, even as a child. He was quiet, serious and respectful, even in the face of a tumultuous family life.

"My parents were separated I don't know how many times," Mark recalls. "Separated and divorced, and he remarried and divorced and married my mother again and divorced. But all that stuff didn't have any effect on me. The love was there from both of them. And this was life."

"I was the kind of kid they didn't have to stay on top of. I knew what my limits were and what was expected of me. I didn't have a whole whale of rules and I had sense enough to know what I couldn't do. I was always the kind of kid who never had to be spanked. It would break my heart to have my parents upset with me. If I knew I had disappointed my parents, I would cry."

CHAPTER TWO

Racing against "green-tooth pulpwood haulers."

Above: The day before his first race Mark posed with the car outside the Julian Martin Trucking garage in Batesville, Arkansas. Over the winter the team transformed the abandoned hulk behind Larry Shaw's Auto Clinic into a beautifully prepared race car. **Left:** March 1974. The 1955 Chevrolet is nearly painted. Still to come is outlining around the "2", underlining of "Larry Shaw's Auto Clinic" and "The Armadillo" nickname in white. To Mark's right is Snake Ellis and Larry Shaw.

One Friday night in the early fall of 1973, at the end of another season of short-track stock car racing at Independence County Speedway in Locust Grove, Arkansas, Julian and Mark were watching a race from the pits.

Julian and Jackie had divorced the previous year, and this was one of the ways father and son spent time together.

Julian loved all speed sports, especially stock car racing. He was a big fan of NASCAR racing and often went to the races at Daytona and Talladega. That year, he had taken Mark to both superspeedways.

During the summer, Julian had bought a share of a late model, V-8 stock car that raced at Independence County Speedway. The track was a quarter-mile dirt oval at the foot of Brock Mountain in the small community of Locust Grove, which is about seven miles southwest of Batesville. Despite its official name, everyone called the track Locust Grove.

Mark had worked in the pits, usually clawing mud from fenders. One afternoon, during a practice session, he had been allowed to drive the car himself. And when it was over, he knew he could handle a stock car. He knew he wanted to race.

The pits at Locust Grove, now called Batesville Speedway, are on a small hill looking over the backstretch. On that fall day in 1973, Mark and his father were standing on the hill. Julian was preoccupied with something else when Mark started badgering him.

"Dad, we gotta build me a race car," Mark said. "We gotta go racing next year."

Julian did his best to ignore his son, who was now fifteen and had just begun his freshman year at Batesville High School.

"Why waste your money on somebody else's car?" Mark demanded. He and his dad should build their own car, he said. And he would drive it.

"Yeah, okay. Okay," Julian said, as much to stop the nagging as anything else.

As far as Mark was concerned, now it was just a matter of time. At fourteen, Mark already had become fast enough on wheels to be a target for the Batesville police. After officers stopped him on his motorcycle several times with no apparent effect, they took a different approach.

"When they'd write him a ticket, they'd write me a ticket, too," Julian says. "And I lost my temper so bad. I'd go down to City Hall, cuss and raise hell and stomp the tickets on the floor. And I told Mark, 'By God, you're either going to have to park that motorcycle or outrun those sons of bitches. Don't bring me another ticket.' So he started outrunning them. He'd cut through yards and get away from them."

But Julian and Jackie would not allow Mark to race motorcycles. Julian had crashed his motorcycle late one night in August, 1971. He had run off a road, and his right leg and arm had hit a concrete post. The wreck had left him with permanent injuries that fifteen operations couldn't fix.

"And while I was in the hospital, Mark had a pretty bad wreck," Julian recalls. "He wound up in the same hospital."

Mark had center-punched a car on his 500cc Honda at an intersection just a couple of blocks from home. That was enough for both parents. They decided their son needed to stop riding motorcycles. When he was fourteen, they bought him a car—a Chevy Blazer.

"That was the deal to get me off motorcycles," Mark remembers. "They would buy me any car I wanted if I quit driving motorcycles. I didn't demand a new car. Buying me a car was simply a convenience to them. They didn't want to drive me around. But when I was finally eligible to get a driver's license, I couldn't have it because I had gotten so many tickets for not having one."

Left: Jackie took her turn posing with the car. She was apprehensive about her son's racing until Julian and Mark showed her the safety features they were building into the car. From that point forward she was enthusiastically behind their project.

Julian had never built an engine until he put together the 235 cubic-inch six-cylinder Chevrolet. Even at this early stage, the engine reflects the team's pride in careful preparation. "Paint and polish helped hide our ignorance," Julian says today.

Troy Lynn Jeffrey

Troy Lynn Jeffrey, Julian's cousin, assembled the drill press the team bought to build the roll cage. He spent countless hours fabricating the first car.

Mark was fifteen, and still too young for a driver's license, when he began pestering his father about building a race car. Soon after his first effort, Mark started nagging him again.

"It's time," he would tell his father. "We need to go work on my car."

Julian had mixed feelings. His trucking company was thriving. He now had several dozen trucks and plenty of work to do. But Julian also was intrigued by the idea of it. And he was comforted by the notion that Mark would quickly give it up. "It'll be all right," he told himself.

In those days, at the few tracks that existed in Arkansas, there were two classes of stock cars—the six-cylinder and the eight-cylinder class. Julian and Mark decided to build a 1955 Chevrolet with a six-cylinder engine. Julian had noticed an abandoned 1955 Chevy in the weeds behind Larry Shaw's Auto Clinic, which was about 200 yards from Julian's truck garage. He bought the hulk from Shaw and towed it back to the truck shop, where he put it in a bay that he rarely used for trucks.

Julian, his cousin Troy Lynn Jeffrey, and Mark started working on the car. They knew nothing about building a race car. But they knew they had to put a roll cage in it. Julian bought some water

Wayne Brooks dominated the six-cylinder stock class in 1974. In exchange for sponsorship from Julian he helped the team build engines and set up the car. He also helped Mark develop his race car driving skills.

pipe, and rented a wire welder, which was better than the stick welder Julian had. They built a substantial roll cage.

"I remember that welder running an awful lot," Mark recalls today.

"It was a pretty heavy car," Julian remembers, "because I put so much bracing in it. He was my little boy and I was scared of him getting hurt. We seated Mark in the center of the car way back towards the back. I didn't want to get him killed and I figured that was the safest place for him."

Jackie Martin didn't say anything when Julian and Mark first mentioned it. She didn't think they were serious.

"When they started building the car, when they started buying parts, I then expressed my concern," she recalls. "Their reaction was, 'Oh, it's not that dangerous.' And in every step they told me what they were doing and how the safety was built in. I just really believed what they were telling me."

As the car began to take shape, it piqued the interest of Larry Shaw, the owner of the nearby auto clinic. Shaw had lunch nearly every day at the Spur Restaurant, which was next to Julian's shop. Once, after Shaw had stopped in, Julian turned to Troy Lynn and said, "Hey, we're getting old Shaw hooked. First thing you know, he'll be up here helping us work on this ol' car."

Not long after, Shaw stopped by again. He walked around the car, studied it, and listened as Julian enthusiastically showed him the latest progress.

"Tell you what I'll do," Shaw announced. "If you put my name on the side of the car, we'll hook the engine up to my Sun (diagnostic) machine before every race."

Julian accepted. And as he predicted, Shaw began working on the car, too.

Shaw recalls: "It was a whole lot more than just tuning that thing up. We worked all winter on that thing. A couple of weeks after I started helping them, someone told Julian that a '55 Chevy station made a better car than what we had. It turns out that the frame was welded better. So we found one and dug it out and sandblasted it and started all over. We didn't know a hell of a lot. Julian ran his trucking place and I had my garage and we had this kid in the ninth grade who wanted to drive a race car. And here we were, getting ready to blow away the world. We worked hard hours. I mean hard hours—a lot harder hours than my little system had been used to. Julian was a trucker, you know. He worked all the time anyway. I wasn't hardly prepared for all of this. So I had to get my system geared a little bit different."

At this early stage, the Mark Martin Racing Team was little more than a backyard, amateur racing project, but with some very dedicated team members. Julian would often work until four AM and then be at the truck shop at seven AM Right from the start, Julian and Mark displayed a single-minded intensity. They were determined to do things right, no matter the cost or effort. It was obsessive perfectionism, pure and simple.

And when they pulled their 1955 Chevrolet race car into the pits at Independence County Speedway in early April, 1974, the bodywork was flawless, and the car was painted in "Hugger Orange", a bright orange hue that gained popularity on Chevrolet Camaros in the late 1960s. The car carried the number two.

The sight immediately left a bad taste in the mouths of some of the racers, especially the rough ones from the sticks who held their cars together with bungee cords and tape. Here was Julian Martin, the rich trucker from Batesville, buying his little boy a brand-spanking-new race car. Anything the boy wants. Well, they were ready for him. Or so they thought.

For Mark, the anticipation had been building all through the winter. He was certain he would race successfully, especially after running those practice laps the year before. He was ready to go.

Right: Mark's first win came in only his second race, held at Locust Grove. His driving position at the center of the car was designed by Julian to protect him from side impacts and intrusions.

Left: Mid-season 1974. Julian guides Mark onto the trailer after photographing the rebodied car behind the Little League field. This pickup's motor was so powerful that it would "bark" the tires shifting from Low to Drive at fifty MPH while towing the race car.

At Locust Grove, the first obstacle was entering a race. Mark was a small kid—five feet tall and just over 100 pounds. He didn't have a driver's license. He was not old enough to drive. He was not even old enough to be in the pits. So Julian and Jackie signed papers giving him permission to drive.

Locust Grove was a tacky, sticky quarter-mile race track, and it was also rough and worn out. It was difficult to drive, and it didn't take many laps for potholes to appear.

At this tiny track, on April 12, 1974, Mark Martin, at the age of fifteen years, three months and three days, started his stock-car racing career. The earliest days of Mark's career are easy to reconstruct because of one remarkable fact: Mark kept a handwritten journal of his first two years. He recorded how he finished and meticulously noted how much money he won and how many points he was awarded. He also wrote a few words about every race.

Mark did not spell every word correctly. He never did spell "Locust Grove" right. First, it was "Locuse," then "Locuste." But what shines through Mark's brief comments is his racing instinct, and the constant turmoil of fender-to-fender competition.

The first entry reads

"Locuse Grove. April 12. Did All right—6,5,2,3. Got 5 points, 56$."

Those words vastly understated the excitement of that day. The most memorable moment came on the second lap, perhaps the third lap, of his first heat race. Mark drove into turn one and, in the traditional style of dirt-track racing, began sawing the wheel back and forth, holding the back end of the car as it slid through the corner. Suddenly, he hit a pot hole. The steering wheel jerked through his hands. Mark lost control. In the pits, Julian and Larry Shaw saw the orange Chevy spin out of sight over the berm of the first turn. There was no retaining fence. Julian had seen plenty of cars go over that bank, but none had ever returned, except on the end of a hook. Julian and Larry looked at each other. Maybe this will cure his racing fever, Julian thought. In the grandstands, Jackie Martin was more captivated than frightened by the sight.

"But the engine never died," she remembers. "And you could just hear him getting in the gas. He just kept going."

Out of sight, Mark fought the wheel. His car tilted to the right on the opposite slope of the bank. But he was determined to get back in the race. "I just got back in control of it, slammed the gas to the floor and drove it back over the bank and kept on racing," he recalls.

From the weeds behind the second turn, Mark drove onto an access road parallel to the back straight and then reentered the track near turn three.

Julian remembers, "When he jumped up over the top and back out on the track, it looked like a dog had jumped out of a hedge bush. Me and Shaw looked at each other and said, 'Lookee here! Look what our boy is doing!' "

YOUNG DRIVER—15-year-old Mark Martin can't get a drivers license but he proved Sunday in races on the Stuttgart Speedway that he could drive. The Batesville driver won the six-cylinder cars' feature race Sunday at Stuttgart. (See story).

Teenage Driver Wins At Stuttgart

A 15-year-old who isn't old enough to get a driver's license was one of two feature race winners in the inaugural races at the Stuttgart Speedway Sunday at the Stuttgart Municipal Airport.

Mark Martin of Batesville drove an orange Chevy to a heat race victory, then came back to win the Sunday feature competition for six-cylinder racers. During a practice run Saturday, Martin's engine was damaged when a broken rod went through the engine block. An overnight trip to Batesville where he and father Julian rebuilt the engine gave enough power to pace Martin to a Sunday victory.

Martin started racing in April on Batesville and Benton dirt tracks. He won Benton's state championsip six-cylinder race this year.

"His parents are crazy," conceded the young driver's father and chief mechanic.

But his mother sounded a less sarcastic note:

"I don't believe there's a great possibility of him getting hurt at this," she said, adding "I've been real proud of him, and of his pit crew...We've all had a lot of fun this summer."

Hunter, who dominated eight-cylinder competition, is the current champion on Fort

Mark finished third in that heat race and was sixth in the feature.

The next day, the team went racing at Heber Springs. But Mark's race ended only moments after it began. His engine blew up on the second lap. Mark was back in action on April 19, at Locust Grove with an engine Julian purchased from Wayne Brooks, the top six-cylinder driver. In his journal, Mark wrote: "Bumped others a lot." But he won his second heat race. It was his first victory. The only mention of it was in his list of finishing positions: 4,1,2,2.

Through April and May, he learned quickly, and his competitors became meaner.

"Heber Springs. April 20. Everyone was too rough, didn't place in money."

"Locuse Grove. April 26. Not a good night. Too sticky for heavy car. 3 points. 33$.

On April 27, 1974, Mark made his first appearance at the Benton Speedbowl, a half-mile dirt track southwest of Little Rock. It was about 100 miles from Batesville. When the team arrived at the pit gate, the officials would not let them in. Mark was too young to be in the pits, they said. "He's our driver!" protested Julian. The promoter, Kenneth Clifton, was summoned. He knew a good promotion when he saw one. Keep him out? Never. Take advantage of his age. Let the boy in, Clifton ordered. From then on, Mark was the "teen-aged racing sensation."

"Locuse. May 3. Good night—2,2,3,3. 9$ a point. 8 points. 72$.

"Locuse Grove, May 10. 3-2-2-4. 6 points 56$.

"Sercey, May 11. First night there. 4-1-2-4. 7 points 35$. total 494.00$

"Sercey, May 18. The car just won't run good enough. I got beat and knock around a lot. 2,2,4,3—7 points. $40.00

Though he had been in less than a dozen feature races, this fifteen-year-old's natural instincts for understanding the performance and handling characteristics of his race car are apparent in his journal entries. But today, more than twenty years later, Mark and Julian look back and marvel at how green they were.

Below: Larry Shaw discovered this copy of Mark's racing journal among some papers he had stored away in a box. The journal was one of the few items that survived an electrical fire that destroyed Shaw's race car shop in February, 1994.

Locuse Grove
April.12. Did All right – 6, 5, 2, 3
got 5 points, 56$

Hebor Springs
April.13 Blew up sacond lap
no points

Locuse Grove
April.19. Bumped others a lot
4, 1, 2, 2 with Brooks Engin
sacond in overall points, 9 points 108$

Hebor Springs
April 20 Every one was too, rough
didn't place in money.

Locuse Grove.
april 26 not a good night, to sticky
for heavy car. 3 points, 33$

Benton
april 27 Fair night, only two races:

By mid-season the shelf in Mark's bedroom was filled with racing trophies. For many years, Mark kept all his trophies but now he prefers to give them to the team, sponsors, or to family and friends. "I'm not into keepsakes," Mark says.

"We didn't know anything," Mark says. "We were totally ignorant. Oh, it was pathetic how stupid we were. For a long time, we won races and were ignorant."

Julian sought help from anyone willing to give it, and he was not shy about asking. He made a point of getting to know Wayne Brooks. Julian sponsored Brooks' car for $1,000 and painted "Martin Trucking Company" on the side. That made it easier to become friends with Brooks and learn what he knew.

Brooks, who still races late model stock cars today, recalls: "Racing was pretty young for us in Arkansas back then. But I had studied my engine work. I had done some things a little before their time on that six-cylinder engine. I had been racing three years, and I had a real dominant car. I could make the engines get more power, and I could make them stay together. So I could pretty much go to the front at will."

Julian says, "I had never rebuilt an engine until that first year of racing. But Wayne let us come down to his shop. We'd go down to his shop every night for, hell, several weeks, and we took an old engine and had him work on it and show us how to work the block and the crankshaft and the pistons and the rods. They showed us how to build a race engine. His old car wasn't complicated at all, but he told me how he'd rigged the suspension on it and I did our original one just about the same way."

Brooks also helped Mark on the track. He told the boy, "If I'm not tied up with somebody else, racin' them, get in behind me and follow me. Go where I go on the track. Watch what I do."

"He was just a boy," Brooks recalls. "And those old cars didn't have power steering. But Mark's progress was just instant. He was ready. It wasn't like you had to drill it. He was a natural. He just needed to know some really basic things—kind of like which direction to go. He'd want to know what he could do to get through traffic better."

One early written account of Mark's first year of racing comes from a Benton Speedbowl program from the spring of 1974:

"Fourteen-year-old (actually fifteen) Mark Martin of Batesville really showed some of the older boys a few things about driving a race car Saturday night. Mark, who looked like he might have to have a booster chair in the car seat, sure knew what it was all about. In the first heat of six-cylinder cars with a field of 13 entries, Mark took third place. Mark also took third place in the 15-lap feature of 21 cars."

Mark and Julian stand beside the car on an August afternoon at Locust Grove. They arrived early to secure their favorite spot in the pits, which was close to the track and to the bushes, the pit's only bathroom facilities.

On June 1, the team headed to Benton for their longest race yet. They saw it as a tune-up for the all-important state championship stock-car races at Benton at the end of the summer.

Larry Shaw recalls: "I think it was a fifty-lap race. It was a real big deal back then. We were settin' sail. And all at once Mark shuts her off. We were trying to figure out what the hell happened. Mark was one mad SOB. He threw his helmet down on the ground."

Mark remembers: "This was a huge event. It felt like we had gone from Grand National to Winston Cup. I was leading this thing and leading it and leading it and leading it, and the car dies. I get out and they look down in the gas tank. And they said it ran out of gas.

"I was furious. And I told 'em: 'If you can't do any better than that, you're going to have to find somebody else to drive this car.' I was appalled. They didn't laugh at the time, but they sure thought that was funny for some stupid kid to be tellin' them that. But I was pretty much a driver by then."

Mark's journal mirrored his fury:

"Us and Wayne showed them how to run. I would have won the feature but I ran out of *gas*."

The word "gas" was underlined four times.

By mid-year, the narrow shelf above the living room couch at Mark's home was filled with trophies. The team was learning, and finding out how difficult racing really was, and how much dedication it took.

"I think our biggest incentive was that we had an outstanding driver and we realized that right away," says Julian. "Had he just been an ordinary run-of-the-mill driver, we probably wouldn't have tried that hard. He'd put up with anything. He would not quit. Our driver was so good and so serious and worked at it so hard, it gave us a lot of incentive to try to put him in something that worked.

"And if you really care about winning, like I do, you would do anything. If Mark came in and we had to work on something that was hot, we did it. We'd burn the hell out of ourselves. You'd put your hands down header tubes that looked like an octopus. And smoke would come off your knuckles. If you're really fired up, you can see it and you can smell it, but you don't feel it. But, hell, it didn't matter. You just did what it took."

Recalls Shaw: "Mark was so good at telling you what he needed in the car. We figured out right away that we could never give him a surprise; we had to be straight up with him. He knew the car so well and he was so serious, you couldn't mess with him."

Right from the beginning, Mark was a contender. He never ran in the back. But he was also acquiring his share of enemies.

"It really wasn't a gentleman's sport back then," says Brooks, who caught his share of grief for winning. "Most of these guys were what I would call 'green-tooth pulpwood haulers.' With some of 'em, you could get your head knocked around if you didn't watch it. It was an accomplishment to simply get out there and *try* to race."

Mark had several strikes against him. He was a boy, and a small one at that. His team came to the track with a nice-looking car. He had a father who could afford what the team needed to succeed. And he won.

"They would pick on him and one guy wrecked him a bunch of times" says Julian. "One time this guy was bumpin' with him and then first thing you know Mark eases up there behind him and if you didn't know for sure you'd think it was an accident the way he just spinned him out. He was an aggressive little cuss."

"Benton, July 6. I got run over by No. 7 on purpose. In the feature, got side tore out of the car. 2,5—35$.

"Benton, Aug. 3. A smoother night than usual. 2,2—80.00$

"Locuse. Aug. 18. Had a very good night but I would have got 1st once when this old car spun out in front of me. 1,2,2,3—10 points -70$.

September 18, 1974

15-Year-Old Wins Two On Arkansas Clay Way

LITTLE ROCK, Ark. — Mark Martin, the 15-year-old rookie who made track history Sept. 11 with his six-cylinder championship win, scored again Saturday night at Bendon Speedbowl, taking the feature checker on the final night of the season.

Martin, starting fourth, took the lead on the first lap and held it for the full 20 fighting off Albert Bryant who ran second. Johnny Brown and Larry Potter were third and fourth.

Brown took a heat with the other going to big John Stacks.

Hubert Cash jumped into first place in the late model stock feature when Larry Carson went wide to avoid a 13th lap spinout. Carson developed engine trouble on the 18th circuit and limped to second ahead of Dave McCoig and Ed Jordan. Cash took a heat as well and veteran Bobby Pruitt took one as well.

"Benton. Aug. 19. Had a fun night. The old Ford man threatened to whip everyone. 3,3—60.00.

"Locust. Aug. 23. Tore out the trans. Got fixed for feature.

Borrowed Albert's tall tires. Wayne got called illegal, so we won the feature. 36.00$ + 25.00$ + 9.00$

On August 31, a rain-out at Benton prompted the team to race at Heber Springs instead. The only problem was their car was equipped with two one-barrel carburetors, and only a single carburetor was allowed at Heber Springs. Right in the middle of the feature race, Mark's hood blew off.

"And those two little chrome carburetors were just shining under the lights," Julian says.

"At that point, our deal was to just get out of there," recalls Shaw. "We didn't care about the money or anything. Mark drove straight into the pits and up on the trailer. And of course, a crowd was gathering around. And they weren't too happy. The crowd was getting bigger and bigger, so we weren't sticking around."

Julian remembers: "In the confusion, they jumped in the hauler and left. And I was still in the pits gathering stuff up. So I got left in the pits with all these mad sons of bitches. I ended up riding back home with one of the ones who was the maddest. But that convinced people all over the countryside that we were illegal. They thought we cheated like that all the time."

"Heber Springs, Aug. 31. We ran two one-barrels and had it made. Then all of a sudden in the feature the hood blows off and everyone sees it!"

On September 6, at Locust Grove, Mark was awarded the high-point trophy for the six-cylinder class. The next week at Benton, he was given the sportsmanship award. Then he went out and beat Brooks by a fender in the feature.

On September 11, 1974, a Wednesday night, Mark and the race team returned to Benton Speedbowl for the state championships.

Recalls Mark: "Fifty laps is a long race for that kind of car at that level. That was like a 600-mile race is today. We always had to start mired up in the field somewhere because they inverted the field (started the slowest in the front). But in this particular race, we didn't start as far back as normal.

The first paved oval in Arkansas was the half-mile Stuttgart Speedway. Mark was there on opening day and won the first race, beating rival Tommy Joe Pauschert. Julian and Larry replaced the car's blown transmission between sessions in eight minutes flat.

"We ran really, really good. There were a lot of cars and a lot of lapped traffic, but I don't remember racing anybody. I won, and I don't know how to describe how big that win was. That wasn't weekly racing, it was a big event. There was a lot of competition on an unfamiliar track under unfamiliar circumstances. It was one of the more outstanding things I have done in my career."

His journal reads:

"We won the Arkansas state championship. A long run. It blew oil and had a busted radiator at the last because of the car that got in my way and I had to spin him out."

By the end of the season, Mark was an experienced dirt-track racer. After the state championship, he had even tried asphalt for the first time at a half-mile track in Stuttgart. "Had a lot of fun, but not as well as dirt," he wrote in his journal.

At Benton Speedbowl alone in 1974, he had entered 101 races and won twenty-two. He finished second in twenty-eight races and third in thirty-six. He placed in all but fifteen. Mark had astounded the small racing fraternity in Arkansas. And he had angered some of them.

But for everyone involved, the lasting memory is how much fun it was.

Jackie recalls: "Mark had a lot of success early on, and that becomes really contagious. It was really a fun time. We were all just really consumed by it and very excited by it. Even talking about it now, I get excited. Racing was really, really new in that part of the country then. It didn't happen around there much. I got hooked that first year. We all did. It not only changed everybody's life around our house, it changed the whole community."

FACES IN THE NEWS — Fifteen-year-old rookie Mark Martin receives the Arkansas Six-Cylinder Championship trophy from Kim Green at the Benton Speedbowl in Little Rock. Young Martin is also high-point man in the class at Independence County Speedway in Locust Grove, Ark. In the center panel, Jon Barr holds his trophy after

Mark is shown on his way to winning the first Arkansas State Championship at the Benton Speedbowl. Thirty-seven drivers started the fifty-lap race, which was much longer than the fifteen-to twenty-lap events Mark had run before. Julian made the note.

State Champ. Night

NAME

NO. _____ AMOUNT _5. 00_

F.I.C.A. _____ ADVANCE _____

FED. W.H. TAX _____ STATE W.H. TAX _____

ALL OTHER _Hobbs_ NET PAY _Net 1_

_441_

Tulsa State Fair
_9-29-74_

"Banking Service
Beyond the Ordinary"

the innovators

**The F&M Bank &
Trust Company**

Telephone 936-1151

1330 SOUTH HARVARD — TULSA, OKLA. 74104

MEMBER FEDERAL DEPOSIT INSURANCE CORPORATION

430-22

Above: The fourth-place prize money—five dollars—from the September 1974 race at the Tulsa State Fair came in this envelope. Mark started thirteenth and worked his way to second before the transmission broke. **Left:** A common sight: Julian working on the car as the sun sets at the Benton Speed Bowl. The bar below the "2" stiffened the body and kept small bumps from damaging the car. It was an aluminum roof bow from a refrigerated trailer.

"My dad and Larry Shaw almost ruined me."

The 1974 racing season was over in Arkansas, but the state championship victory had so electrified Mark and the team, they weren't ready to quit. Julian had noticed an ad in *National Speed Sport News* for a race at the Tulsa State Fair on September 29. Julian called the track to make sure he could enter a six-cylinder car.

"Anything up to 292 (cubic inches) is legal," the promoter told Julian. The promoter didn't bother to say that the other racers would be running with V-8 engines. And the team didn't find that out until they arrived at the fairgrounds after driving almost 300 miles.

Remembers Shaw: "We knew right off that we were in bad, serious trouble out there that day."

But Mark put on a show, at least while he lasted. Saddled with an underpowered six-cylinder engine, Mark raced around the five-eighths mile Tulsa track in second gear, putting an enormous strain on the transmission. He used second gear on quarter-mile tracks. It was not recommended for a five-eighths mile dirt track, but it gave him the torque needed to compete with the V-8s.

He started thirteenth, and immediately began passing cars. On the twelfth lap, he was running in second when the flywheel broke and the transmission snapped. His race was over. And his season was over as well.

During the cold Arkansas winter, as Mark and his father and Larry Shaw reflected on their first season, they knew they had become a team. They remembered the race at Stuttgart when Mark's transmission was about to fail.

Replace body sheet metal with new each time it gets bent; pit Crew call themselves Bushes Bros. Woods Bros. have fastest pit crew in world, we are coming on;

With Larry perched in one window and Julian in the other, Mark had circled through the pits while they listened to him shift gears. Sure enough, it was failing. On the spot, they changed the transmission. Mark had timed them. Eight minutes.

Julian says: "We just had him sit in the car and we changed it and got him out and he didn't even miss a heat race."

They were fast, just like the Wood Brothers in NASCAR racing, who had perfected the lightning pit stop in the 1960s. That year, the Wood Brothers Ford, driven by David Pearson, had won seven races. Julian held the Woods in high admiration.

"So we got to thinking about it and I said, 'Ol' Leonard Wood, he's probably

down there in Virginia looking over his shoulder right now. They don't know who we are, but we're coming. If they're the Wood Brothers, then we're the Bushes Brothers.'"

They began calling themselves the "Bushes Brothers Race Team." They had T-shirts made up, and they painted the moniker on the side of their car.

By Thanksgiving of 1974, work was underway on a new car for the 1975 season. The bare chassis of another 1955 Chevrolet sat on jack stands in Julian's truck shop.

"It was definitely important for us to build another car because we had learned so much that first year," Mark recalls. "The first car we built was a blacksmith's wonder. The second car was a much nicer car. This was a real race car."

Mark and Julian took their new chassis to Springfield, Missouri, where Larry Phillips, one of the top short-track stock-car drivers in the midwest, welded a roll cage onto it. Mark was thrilled by his first visit to a professional race shop. It was also his first meeting with Phillips, who would come to play an important role in his early racing life, both on and off the track.

The roll cage Phillips installed on the chassis was no home-welded contraption made of heavy water pipe, like the cage on their first race car. Phillips used O-95 steel tubing, which was lighter and thinner but plenty strong. The 1975 car had other refinements as well. The driver's seat was moved from the center of the car to its standard position. The dashboard was meticulously hand-indexed, a reflection of the team's obsessive attention to detail, and long winter nights of labor. The suspension was built with weight jacks in the rear, so Julian could add or remove "wedge" to adjust the weight load of each wheel. The car also had a new, lower front end to allow Mark to take the car lower through the corners.

During that first season, the team had spent many hours cleaning mud off the car between races.

"I bet some days we took 200 pounds off the car at Locust Grove," remembers Julian. "It was old clay and it was hard and it was really difficult to dig out. And about the only way you could do it was with your fingers. It was a tough job. Nobody else did it. Most of the guys didn't do much except cool off. But we thought that cleaning the mud off was a big thing."

Recalls Larry: "The second year, Julian figured out a deal for that. He made some fender panels. That made it a lot simpler. That took care of a lot of mud digging."

To learn more about race cars and engines, Julian bought several technical racing books published by Steve Smith. "Everything I could find to read, I read," Julian says.

The most useful book was "Racing Engine Preparation," published in 1975 by Smith and veteran NASCAR engine builder Waddell Wilson. It was a step-by-step guide on how to build a stock-car racing engine. Julian's copy soon became dog-eared, heavily underlined, and smeared with grease. Late at night, after Mark and Larry had gone home, Julian would sometimes roll underneath the car on his creeper and just stare at the engine, thinking about ways to increase power and reduce friction.

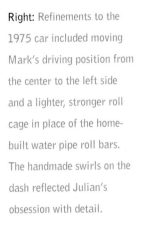

Right: Refinements to the 1975 car included moving Mark's driving position from the center to the left side and a lighter, stronger roll cage in place of the home-built water pipe roll bars. The handmade swirls on the dash reflected Julian's obsession with detail.

"I learned an awful lot from that book," Julian says.

Larry says: "Julian would read 'em and I'd take one home that he wasn't reading. And that's really how we got a whole lot of our information. It was like going to school."

Julian also experimented with fuel. "The second year, I got to mixin' some exotic fuels that were not legal," Julian says. "I was afraid they would blow up and burn my damn place down, so I kept the stuff out in the weeds some distance from the building. I'd buy benzene by the barrel and I had a bunch of ingredients. And I'd go out there in the weeds and draw it out and mix it up. I'd mix and test, mix and test. I don't remember where I learned how to do it. I think I read it somewhere.

"And I'd mix that stuff up and, boy, it would make that ol' car yodel. Benzene is really dry, so I put castor oil in it to give it a little lubrication. That also made it smoke a little. So it gave our competitors hope that maybe we were going to blow up. I added just a little more castor oil for that effect."

By the time the season started on April 5, 1975, at Benton Speedbowl, everyone was raring to go, especially Mark.

"It was just like we had him caged up all winter. He was ready to race," Larry says.

But the first race of that season was a cold dose of reality, as Mark reported in his racing journal.

"The suspension was too stiff for the dirt. Got our doors blew off. And body beat all to hell 4- 5 - 6. 1 point. 10$."

A week later, on the asphalt at Stuttgart, Mark finished second in three consecutive races to a nineteen-year-old driver from Carlisle, Arkansas, named Tommy Joe Pauschert.

Pauschert ran with the number 10-4. A decal on the side of his car read, "The Desperado."

"April 12. Stuttgart. The suspension was very close to right... Had a lot of fun and pushed 10-4 all the way around the track but couldn't pass. 2-2-2 1 40$."

But on April 26, in a raucous night at Benton Speedbowl, Mark turned the tables.

"57C and 10-4 led, but on the last #4 turn, I got a slingshot on 57C and won the race. I led the feature all the way and got tore down for winning the feature because they couldn't stand getting beat."

Below: November 1974. The frame was prepared inside Julian's truck shop for the new, improved race car for the 1975 season. The team sanded, polished and welded all the seams before assembling the chassis.

11-22-74   #2 - 1975 Car.

The 1975 engine was built using tips Julian and Larry Shaw learned by reading engine-building books. Note the dual carburetors with chrome air cleaners that had nearly started a riot at Heber Springs the summer before.

Other racers had passed the hat and collected $100 to protest Mark's victory in the twenty-lap feature. He had started third and run away with the race, lapping the field. Pauschert had spun out, but finished second.

No one had evidence that his car did not conform to the rules, but he had beaten them so badly they were convinced he had to be cheating. He was awarded the $100 protest fee after his car passed the inspection, but it was a lot of work dismantling the engine and putting it back together. And it was a sign of the contentiousness to come that season.

"It was unbelievable," remembers Julian. "I shouldn't have been so surprised, but I just couldn't believe that they resented it as bad as they did being beat by a kid."

Mark and Pauschert waged their personal duel at several Arkansas tracks, including Benton, Locust Grove, and Des Arc. If Mark didn't win, Pauschert did. Mark won more than half of his races. He reported in his journal that he won 51 of 96 races (including 20 of 32 features) in 1975, and finished second 32 times.

WITH FLAG IN HAND — Mark Martin, 16, of Batesville carries the checkered flag around the Independence County Raceway track after winning the Mid-Season Championship Race in the six cylinder class Friday. A protest against Martin's car was registered, but it was found to be legal. Wayne Brooks of Bald Knob won the feature race in the eight cylinder division.

In April, the *Arkansas Democrat* ran its first article about Mark, headlined "A Vet at Sixteen."

Mark said he wanted to follow in the footsteps of Richard Petty and Bobby Allison. "This year I spent as much as five nights a week until midnight working on our car," he told reporter Teri Thompson. "It has paid off because last year we had a lot of engine trouble and breakdowns. This year we're running strong and the car has almost been perfected."

Wrote Thompson: "Veteran observers at the Benton track say Mark, despite his age, is by far the most professional driver in the six-cylinder class. He is also the hardest worker, spending most of his free time working on his car."

Despite his success in 1975, Mark had no landmark victories like his 1974 state championship. The thing he remembers most about 1975 is how rough and full of trouble it was, particularly early in the year.

Mark says, "I don't remember that much about 1975 other than not being appreciated, people not liking us, getting tired of us winning and saying ugly things."

Recalls Larry Shaw: "We were out at Locust Grove one night and our motor blew up right in the middle of the race. Mark coasted into the infield and a lot of people in the stands just cheered. We had been winning so much, they were glad to see us break and fall out. Boy, I mean it just absolutely broke my heart. I didn't feel like those people realized how hard we were working."

But that treatment went hand-in-hand with winning.

Recalls Wayne Brooks, another consistent winner, "I had been protested so many times, I was wearing the head bolts out tearing apart the motor. They made jokes like, 'You've got

a zipper on your motor.' Heck, some of them were using illegal motors and they couldn't even see my back bumper, so they just *knew* I was illegal. You'd drive through the pits and some of them would give you the finger. When Mark came along, he just jumped right in those shoes."

Mark's team, to be sure, didn't make it easier on him. His nature, off the track, was to be quiet, polite and humble. Julian and Larry were exactly the opposite.

"My dad and Larry Shaw, those two were the biggest smart-alecks on the face of the earth," Mark says. "You're a product of your environment and some of it rubbed off on me. They almost ruined me. They were terrible."

Julian says, "We were a couple of smart asses. We probably brought a lot of it on ourselves."

Even Brooks, their ally in 1974, became an enemy. In 1975, Brooks had sold all of his six-cylinder equipment to Julian and promised he wouldn't compete in the six-cylinder class. He began racing eight-cylinder stock-cars. But he had a miserable debut in February at the World Series of Asphalt Racing at New Smyrna Speedway in Florida. He returned to Arkansas broke. So he agreed to build a six-cylinder engine for the Pauscherts. That in-furiated Julian. He was well aware of Brooks' skill as an engine builder, and he felt that Brooks had reneged on his promise not to

compete against them. Brooks believed that he had promised only not to *drive* against Mark.

On the underside of the hood of Mark's car, Julian painted this message: "WE built this son-of-a-bitch. Gimlet 'ass' Brooks didn't have anything to do with it!"

Mark's journal described other troubles:

> In his first appearance of the year at Locust Grove on May 9, he "started dead last every race and won all 4 of them," he wrote. But: "We had to change our A-frames because of [a protest by] Jimmy Grubbs."

On May 16 in a heat race at Locust Grove, "Grubbs tried to run me off the track, but I spun him out twice and we got black flagged," Mark wrote. He won the feature.

The next day, at Benton, "Q28 put me in the mud hole in the first heat." He won the second heat. In the feature, he was on Pauschert's bumper as they moved through the field. "He run onto some traffic and got out of shape and I tapped him and I went around (him) and he went crazy and ran over everything," Mark wrote.

Except for this single entry, Mark wrote of no other problems with Pauschert on the track. Today, he remembers no problems. Most of the time, they managed to race hard and run close without trouble.

"I tell you how good those two were," says Brooks. "You could take the rest of the cars off the track and put those two boys out there and see one heck of a show. In those days, it wasn't a matter of who was going to win. It was a matter of who was going to finish third. And there were several nights when they lapped the third-place car. Looking back, I think that was probably the best thing that ever happened to Mark that year. He had to be on his toes. He had to learn to use his head."

The crews, however, hated each other.

At Des Arc on May 26, the tension boiled over into a brawl. Mark described it as a "gang fight."

Recalls Shaw:

"Somehow or another, when we was going for the lead, Tommy Joe got into the front straight-away wall. Back then, I was always grinning for no reason. And (Pauschert) come off the track and went and told his dad that I was down there grinnin.' Well, hell, they all came down and we had a free-for-all. When it was all said and done, there was about twenty different fights going on."

Larry Shaw (left) and Steve Looney pose in the car. Note the larger, wider outside tire compared to the narrower driver's side tire. This exaggerated tire stagger helped the car to turn left more easily.

The crew before a race. From left to right: Larry Shaw; Julian; Marty Adelotte, Mark's schoolmate and friend; Steve Looney; and Larry's brother-in-law, Jackie Rounds. The patch on Larry's shirt identifies the team as the 1974 Arkansas State Champions.

Julian says: "It was like a pile-up at a football game. Hell, people came from every direction, jumping in there."

When Mark won on July 4 at Locust Grove, his competitors protested once again.

"It cost $125 to protest," says Julian. "Someone would go through the pits and each one of 'em would pitch in ten dollars. So we'd have to work all night tearing the engine apart to show 'em it was legal."

Mark's car was ruled legal on July 4, but the team decided it was no longer worth the trouble to race at Locust Grove.

"We'll avoid a hassle if we can, and we can avoid one by not running at Locust Grove," Mark told *Batesville Guard* Sports Editor Larry O'Dell that summer. "And that's the bad part about it. It's my own hometown track." "At Benton," he said, "They love us, and we love them."

So they spent most of the rest of the season racing at Benton. In the state championship race, Mark won the pole. Late in the race, "the SOBs started playing ping pong with me," Mark wrote in his journal. "Left mad, so we were disqualified." Today, neither he, Julian or Larry remember the details. It was a letdown from 1974.

Overall, the 1975 season had been just as successful as 1974. There was nothing left to be accomplished in the six-cylinder class. There was no question about what to do for 1976. It was time to build a late model stock car with a V-8 engine.

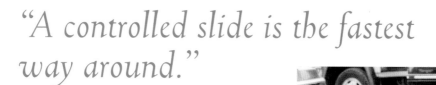

CHAPTER FOUR

"A controlled slide is the fastest way around."

When the 1976 racing season opened in mid-April at Independence County Raceway in Locust Grove, Mark and his team arrived with the late-model, V-8 Camaro they had built over the winter. The chassis was welded at Larry Phillips' shop in Springfield, Missouri. The team then brought it back to Batesville, where they hung the body. They put the number two on it, of course, and they painted it Hugger Orange.

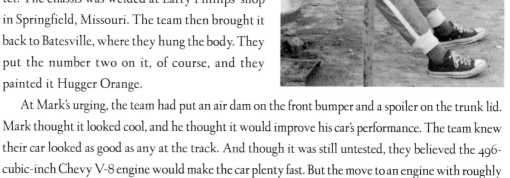

At Mark's urging, the team had put an air dam on the front bumper and a spoiler on the trunk lid. Mark thought it looked cool, and he thought it would improve his car's performance. The team knew their car looked as good as any at the track. And though it was still untested, they believed the 496-cubic-inch Chevy V-8 engine would make the car plenty fast. But the move to an engine with roughly three times the power of the six-cylinder was a big step up, and fraught with problems.

Mark won his first heat race at Locust Grove on opening night, but he did not place in the feature.

"It was hard enough that it took me about three or four nights of racing to get pretty good at it,"

Left: This photo taken at Locust Grove shows the controlled slide Mark holds to set up a pass. The front wheels are turned dramatically to the right to check the slide and keep the car turning left.

Above: Mark collected his thoughts while resting on the tail of the team's hauler between races at Wynne Stadium.

Mark recalls. "The car was really heavy. It had tons of horsepower and it didn't have power steering. I was little and I had trouble keeping up with the car for a couple of races. And then we put power steering on it."

Julian, Larry and Mark found a power-steering assembly at a local junk yard and installed it themselves.

Mark says: "We were not very good engineers. So putting power steering on the race car was very hard. It wasn't just bolt-on. It was a lot of work. But, boy, it was nice. Once we got in on there, I could really go."

"We had to get a lot of things worked out," Mark says. "We had rear panhard bar heim joints that would break all the time, until we finally got some aircraft-grade heim joints. And the rear springs had a tendency to fall out of the car while I was racing. I thought we were going to get whipped one night because a guy brought a spring over that had fallen out of our car and hit his. We didn't even know it fell out."

But Mark's skill at controlling his car soon reached new levels. Larry Shaw remembers a race at Ida, Arkansas, where Mark literally ran up onto the track's concrete wall. "One set of tires ended up on the wall and the other down on the track," he says. "The flagman had to jump back to avoid being hit. Mark never cracked the throttle, and he never lost it as he was coming off the wall."

At West Plains, there was a particularly treacherous earthen bank that served as the outer wall. All the locals warned against getting near the berm. It had destroyed many cars. But Mark went out and rode up on it with his right rear wheel at full speed.

"He passed the track favorite up there to lead on the outside," Julian recalls. "The people that

Left: Although the team bought the tube-frame chassis, it still took an enormous amount of work to build the car. Mark did much of it himself, including welding.

Below: The 496 cubic-inch V-8 had almost three times the power of the six-cylinder engine and took some getting used to. But after a few races, Mark had adapted his driving style. His driving skills rose to a new level.

The Camaro's tidy interior shows the team's uncommon attention to detail. The red line of tape at the top of the steering wheel provides a reference point for when the wheels are positioned straight ahead.

raced there all the time said it couldn't be done. He didn't know that, so he did it."

On July 17, the team headed to the Bolivar Speedway in southwest Missouri to race some of the top drivers in the region. Mark did not expect to win. He only wanted to see how he would stack up against better drivers, now that he was comfortable in his new late-model stock car.

"The guys at Bolivar had reputations throughout a whole region," Mark says. "Ken Essary had a bounty on him that year because he was never beat. The promoter would bring in somebody to try to beat him. These were the guys who had bigger reputations for being better racers and smarter racers, and having better cars."

Mark doesn't remember winning the first heat race. "But I do remember running second in the B feature," he says. "See, I couldn't even make the A feature unless I ran first or second in the B feature."

Early in the B feature, one car tumbled down the backstretch, and another car slammed into the flipping vehicle while it was in the air.

"All of them were wrecking and wild and driving like idiots," Mark remembers. "I couldn't get in there and race because those people were running over each other and turning over, so I ran second." He had to pass another car on the final lap to do it. And he also had to forfeit his B feature winnings for the privilege of starting last in the feature.

Mark started from the back and began a mad charge toward the front. On the twelfth of twenty-five laps, he took the lead.

"Now this thing is building up pretty wild," he says. "I remember passing cars and passing cars and passing cars. It was definitely one of the most unbelievable things. I just couldn't believe I was fixin' to win."

Essary was on his bumper throughout the final thirteen laps, vainly trying to find a way to pass. The crowd was in a frenzy.

"People were climbing up the fence," Mark recalls. "It was the wildest thing. I beat people that I thought were some of the greatest racers in the United States, and we just barely even got in the race. It was a pretty big deal. To go up there and beat them when we didn't know diddley, I absolutely do not understand to this day how we did it, but we did. We beat people we had no business beating and we had no idea how we beat them. And those greatest wins were always that way."

Julian recalls: "Mark and I got to working pretty good together. I could watch him run and see how the car was doing, especially on dirt, and adjust the suspension between races. A lot of times he didn't even have to tell me what it was doing. I could see it. So I'd watch him and work on the car a little between each heat race and by the time we ran the feature, boy, we'd kill."

New sponsors appeared on the trunk lid. The aluminum blanks carefully riveted in place of tail lights are another example of the team's meticulous attention to detail.

"Mark could tell you right quick what kind of race car he needed," recalls Larry. "You didn't have to do a bunch of testing or wondering. And back then everybody would go around to see what right-rear spring you had on, or what sway bar, or this and that. Mark never did. He didn't want to know. As best I remember, we never did run in the back in any place we ever went to. And we had a chance of winning most of the time."

Julian recalls, "Shaw could really get something done quick. He wasn't really precise on a lot of things. It might not be the precision job Mark or I would have done. But it was in the neighborhood. And by God, if you needed something done in a hell of a hurry, stuff like that was Shaw's strong

For 1976 the race car transporter was rebodied with a ramp-back. By the middle of the season, the race car's smooth bodywork and curves would be a mass of dents and the fender wells would be cut away.

point. And the stuff was hot. It burned you just to touch it. There wasn't any way to avoid it."

On the track, Mark was having a blast driving his car on dirt with its awesome V-8 power.

"I liked to slide the car," Mark says. "That was fun. Most of the tracks we ran were tacky, muddy race tracks and we ran pretty crossways in the corners. The dry, slick, black race tracks we tended to drive the cars straighter on. It was more like running on ice. But on a tacky, muddy race track, right before you got to the corner, you turned the steering wheel nearly backwards, and you mashed the gas wide open, and controlled the car with the throttle and the steering wheel. A controlled slide was the fastest way around."

Late in 1976, Mark made his debut at the Fairgrounds Speedway in Springfield, Missouri, the home track of Larry Phillips. It was a half-mile asphalt oval, but Mark took his dirt car. It was the only car he had.

Phillips so dominated the track that the promoters hired top regional and national drivers to race against him. The night Mark raced, NASCAR Winston Cup star Donnie Allison was the hired gun. Both remember their first encounter.

Allison: "When I talked to him, he told me his ambition was to get in NASCAR. And I remember telling him that it takes a lot of hard work and even more determination to make it. And he said, 'Well, I'm not afraid to work. And I'm determined.'

"Of course, I've heard that a lot. And very few of them make it. But I was very impressed with him at the time. Here Mark was out there, just a little bitty guy, driving this real big race car. He was determined."

Allison had less regard for Mark's car. The gaping wheel openings for dirt tracks were obviously out of place on the asphalt track, and Mark was embarrassed.

"You sure you've got enough fenderwell clearance there, son?" Allison asked Mark, who was mortified.

Larry laughs: "You could have run an antelope over the tops of our tires between the wheel and the fender well."

"It was kind of shabby—typical of the stuff I saw at the time," Allison recalls. "Of course, while it may not have been the prettiest thing cosmetically, it raced well."

"Donnie was real friendly," Mark says. "The Allisons were always real good to me, even in the beginning. They treated me like somebody when they didn't know who I was."

In the race, Phillips, Allison, and Mark started in the back. All three came through the pack in three laps. And for the next twenty-seven laps, Phillips led Allison around the oval, with Mark doggedly keeping up, straining his car to the limit. On the thirty-first lap, Mark's engine blew up. As he parked his car, the crowd gave him a tremendous ovation. Phillips went on to win, but the Springfield fans had gotten a taste of the future.

Mark Martin of Batesville wins Tri-State championship

LOCUST GROVE — Mark Martin of Batesville, driving his Bushes Brothers Camaro, captured the Tri-State Championship at Independence County Speedway here Saturday night.

Martin, Victory Lane magazine's driver of the year and the local speedway's high point winner, took the lead on the 20th lap and fought off the charge of Ken Essary of Galena, Mo., in car 55.

Don Hester of Tupelo, Miss., took the checkered flag for the Friday night feature race. Essary was his biggest threat throughout the race. Martin led much of the way, but was forced out of the race in a wreck.

"The races were some of the most exciting of the year," track co-owner James Isaacs said, "and the management wishes to thank all those who made the fine season possible."

Here are the results of the two weekend feature races:

Friday night — Hester, first, ar 327; Essary, second, car 55; Jerry Inman, third, car D-7; Ted Fink, fourth, car 147; Greg Herron, fifth, car 30; Burl McGee, sixth, car A1; Johnny Bole, seventh, car 12; Carl Williams, eighth, car 16; Shelby Henderson, ninth, car 66; Ed Jordan, 10th, car 60.

Saturday night — Martin, first, car 2; Essary, second, car 55; Roger Chism, third, car 8; McGee, fourth, car A1; Vance Cook, fifth, car 31; Bud Perkey, sixth, car 32; Fink, seventh, car 147; Darrell Mooneyham, eighth, car 20; Herron, ninth, car 30; Glen Hines, 10th, car 12.

To his competitors and the fans, Mark had become "The Kid." The nickname stuck with him for many years. Mark won dozens of races in 1976, including the Mid-Season Championship, a fifty-lap race at Locust Grove. He took the lead after a driver named Jerry Inman crashed, tumbling end over end through the first turn.

The team's Labor Day weekend schedule was typical of racing that year. On Saturday, Mark won the feature at Wynne Stadium in Heber Springs. On Sunday, Mark finished seventh in a fifty-lap race at Monett, Missouri, billed as the Four-State Championship. On Monday night, at another fifty-lapper at Mo-Ark Speedway in West Plains, Missouri, Mark led every lap.

At the end of the season, Mark won the Tri-State Championship, a special year-end race at Locust Grove that drew the best regional drivers, including Ken Essary, who finished second, dogging Mark in the final laps. By now, he had a fan club. It was organized in 1976 by Batesville friends Rusty and Mary Amos, who took the trouble to put an ad in the local newspaper. "Mark Martin Fan Club Is Now Organizing," the ad read. "Come On Fans If Mark Is Your Favorite V-8 Stock Car Driver Join Now."

Victory Lane, a weekly racing newspaper published in Springfield, had an annual contest for driver of the year, and Mark's fan club members flooded the newspaper with votes. He won by a sizable margin over Larry Phillips.

Mark won the points championship at Locust Grove and at Wynne Stadium. He won twenty-seven feature races in 1976, and finished first, second or third in all but twelve of his ninety-seven races.

Other drivers said Mark was a clean and skillful racer, according to an article in the *Batesville Guard*. One of them, Larry Carson, said, "Mark has a steady style. He is very consistent. He runs his car for all that it is worth, and stays on top of all situations. He is aware of what is going on all around the track, not just what is in front and behind him. Mark is a real good sportsman. When something goes wrong, he usually blames himself instead of one of the other drivers."

Left: Mark, standing in the center, is clearly the youngest competitor in the pit area. Right: Mark's first fan club was organized by Batesville friends, Rusty and Mary Amos, who painted their van in the team colors.

CHAPTER FIVE

Above: The trophy girl at the Tri-State Speedway in Fort Smith, Arkansas, gave Mark the driver of the month trophy for April, 1977. "By then he'd grown up and aged a lot", Julian says. "I'm afraid his aging process started much, much too early. I never treated him like a boy, but always like a man." **Left:** The weather for the 1977 State Championship race at Fort Smith was very hot. Many teams used relief drivers during the 250-lap event because their regular drivers suffered from heat exhaustion. Mark drove the whole race and revived with a drink as he talked with Julian.

"We drank it instead of spraying it."

As 1976 slipped into 1977, Mark, Julian, and Larry were building yet another race car. The chassis was made by Ed Howe, the best short-track car builder at the time. The team had decided to move from dirt tracks to asphalt tracks, so once again they faced uncharted territory.

The team spent long nights that winter trying to produce the perfect car. But first they had to learn the peculiarities of an asphalt car. They made mistakes, and would sometimes have to tear apart the product of hours of labor and do it over.

"I'd work in there until I didn't know whether it was night or day," Julian says. "And I'd be surprised that it was daytime, or nighttime, when I finally walked out."

Finally, the car was finished—an orange and white Camaro with a black hood. It was their fourth car. They took it to Ed Howe's shop in Michigan so Howe could show them how to set it up.

"I went with my dad," Mark recalls. "The car repulsed Howe and his guys so badly, they humiliated us. They almost wouldn't speak to us. When we put the car on their scales, it was ridiculously

Julian stood beside Mark's Camaro at New Smyrna Beach, the first event of the 1977 season. Despite the team's careful preparation, chassis-builder Ed Howe ridiculed the car as too pretty, too heavy and overengineered. "It was pretty tough to kill ourselves all winter and then hear that," says Julian.

heavy. They were weight freaks, which we wound up being, too. The car was also too nice. They liked junky, hacked-up stuff. They said it was over-engineered. They made fun of everything."

Recalls Howe: "Yeah, I guess I probably did mention to 'em that I didn't care how pretty it was, just make it fast. They didn't realize that if it was heavier, it was slower. They did really nice, neat work, but I wanted them to go fast."

Mark says: "They showed us how to set it up and we took it back home. And before we raced it, we got aluminum cylinder heads and a lot of other lightweight stuff and we changed things around and got it a lot lighter."

"We came back to Arkansas and we put this thing on a diet," recalls Larry. "Like the header bolts. They're three quarter-inch long. We cut a quarter inch off them. We cut every bolt in the race car. We cut bolts for two or three days and four or five pounds is all we got off."

Julian bought lighter wheels, which meant axle and hub modifications. He found lighter cylinder heads for the engine, a small block Chevrolet V-8. And he flew his plane into the teeth of a blizzard on a Sunday night, with ice already on the ground, to pick them up in Mena, Arkansas.

Julian prepares to unload the car as the team arrives at Fairgrounds Speedway in Springfield, Missouri. From left is Art Hamlett, Julian's brother-in-law; crew member Claude Reed; Julian and his sister, Marilyn Hamlett; and Jackie with Julian's parents, Clyde and Robbie.

Right: After winning the 1977 State Championship at Fort Smith, Mark walked to the team's pit. His right foot was wrapped in duct tape to help insulate it from high temperatures around the firewall and transmission tunnel.

"I don't know why in the hell I didn't wait until Monday or something, but we had to do it now," Julian recalls. "It was a major deal. We had worked all winter on the car. It was almost race time. And we decided to do all this."

The winter preparation time was shortened considerably by Mark's insistence that he run in the World Series of Asphalt Stock-Car Racing for nine nights in February at New Smyrna Speedway in Florida, just ten miles south of Daytona.

"What better way to get pavement experience than to jump into the World Series of Asphalt Racing?" Mark asks. "This was our first year on asphalt, and they run nine nights in a row at New Smyrna."

"It was a hell of a place," remembers Julian. "I can't imagine why in the hell we ever let him con us into starting his asphalt career in that World Series. Everybody has been off for a few months and they're rammy and wild."

Mark says, "The very first night, we took this car out and I didn't qualify well. I started in the back, and when the green flag came out, all of these guys wrecked in front of me coming off turn

two. I killed the car. I bent the frame and everything. I'd never bent a frame before."

The team took the wrecked car to a local shop whose owner was a Howe chassis dealer. Howe, who was at New Smyrna, agreed to look it over.

Howe told Julian: "Well, it's bent. And it probably ain't going to work good. You can't even figure out how to try to set it up. But you can put it back together and get back out there and get the boy a little bit of experience. That's all you're down here for anyway, right?"

Today, Howe remembers how dedicated the Bushes Brothers team was: "You could tell they were workers and were going to do whatever it took to get the job done. A lot of people, when they come to get their car set up, they do what you tell them and they're not really intent on knowing why. But they wanted to know *why* we did everything. They were dead serious."

They missed two nights of racing, working nearly around the clock to fix the car. And when they went back to the track, Julian picked a pit stall at the far upper end of the track.

"We had a little 'ol boy there, we didn't know anything and I was scared, so I didn't even want to pit close to anybody else," Julian says.

Mark qualified third in his first race back. That brought Howe all the way up pit road. He walked slowly around the car, looked it over carefully and then pronounced: "I'll tell you one thing. If this car runs as good in the race as he qualified, I may just have you all bring it up to my place and put it back on my jig. And I'll just change my jig to fit this car."

Mark ran in the top five every night for the rest of the series. He finished sixth in the points. And when the 1977 season opened at Fairgrounds Speedway in Springfield, Missouri, with a Sunday afternoon program on April 3, Mark was ready to challenge the all-powerful Larry Phillips.

But Mark finished fifth in his debut. The car wasn't right. The team headed home with a long list of things to do. They put new brakes on the car, switched to a different brand of tires, and reset

the suspension. When Mark returned the next Sunday, he faced even tougher competition. Wisconsin driver Tom Reffner, the winningest short-track racer in 1975, was in town to do battle with Phillips.

Mark and Phillips battled door to door in the third heat

Left: At Fairgrounds Speedway, Mark and Larry Phillips battle side-by-side through a turn. Mark controlled the track's points championship throughout the season.

race before Phillips edged him at the line. In the trophy dash, Mark dueled with Reffner in another great battle, and won. The crowd gave him a standing ovation—something promoter Max Speak could not recall ever happening before.

In the feature, Mark took the lead on the fifth of thirty laps and stayed there the rest of the way.

On April 22, 1977, Mark battled Dave Watson, the defending track champion at Springfield, in a two-car duel that lasted the entire race, all 75 laps. Mark could bump Watson, but was unable to pass. Watson won by less than a car length.

Phillips was on his bumper the whole way, and Reffner was right behind Phillips. The crowd went wild.

"We had no problems," Phillips said after the race. "We just got outrun."

The Springfield fans had a young, new hot shot to challenge Phillips, and they showed their appreciation.

"In two weeks of racing at the fairgrounds, Mark has become one of the track's most popular young drivers," motorsports writer Kirby Arnold wrote in the *Springfield News and Leader*.

Recalls Julian: "One of the absolutely greatest things—one of the biggest thrills—about our racing is when we started going to the fairgrounds in Springfield. Nobody had beaten Phillips in years, it

seemed like, and Mark is a good, clean, innocent-looking kid. And he starts beating Phillips. You can imagine how the crowd handled that. One time, we had a wreck on the way up there and got there late. They had already been out there practicing. And I guess the crowd was thinking we weren't going to make it. When we came in, you had to ride across the track. So they stopped practice to let us across. And the crowd went crazy."

But Mark knew from experience to be cautious about basking in the limelight. He told Arnold: "If I win every feature this season, then I'd get all sorts of boos. But there's no way that could happen anyway. I know Larry Phillips and he won't have that. He'll have things straightened out next week."

Today, Phillips recalls, "His fan following was enormous because they already have a guy—me—who everybody hates, or at least half the people hate. Mark was everybody's idol, especially with him being a youngster and his mild manner. Mark had a little different style that he'd run on the track. It was a little wider line. Coming off the corners, he was just right against the fence. He just used every bit of the race track. A couple of times, he outran me like this. And I thought I'd better follow him. I never did feel comfortable with it but it was fast."

Five days after his first victory, Mark won again, even more spectacularly. He beat Larry Schuler by a fender after making a daring pass on the final turn. Schuler was the country's most successful short-track driver in 1976.

"It was an almost unheard-of move around the outside of Schuler that Martin executed on the half-mile oval, and it even gave Martin a scare," Kirby Arnold wrote in the *News and Leader* the next day.

"I couldn't get around him underneath and I was afraid to go over him," Mark told Arnold. "But I got brave enough to go ahead."

Through that spring, Mark raced on Friday nights in Springfield and on Saturday nights at Tri-State Speedway in Fort Smith, Arkansas, where Phillips also dominated. Mark quickly took the points lead at both tracks. It was a glorious spring of racing.

After every race in Springfield, the team stopped at a Denny's restaurant. Sometimes, Julian was too wound up about the evening's racing to eat. And when Julian couldn't eat, something else was bound to happen. One night, after Mark had lost a race because of ignition failure, Julian was again too upset to eat. Finally, he left the table. In the middle of the Denny's parking lot, he went after the ignition box, cursing and beating it with a tire iron until his hands hurt too much to continue.

"Man, if you really care about winning, when you leave a race track, even if you got second, you just feel like you've had the life all stomped out of you," Julian says. "I believe I'd rather lose a joint off a finger and win than to be whole and come in second. I'll fight until I'm dead. It's just the way I am and I'm glad I'm like that. It's not comfortable being around someone like me."

Another night, after Mark had caused Phillips to crash, Julian wasn't interested in food. He wasn't angry, he was brooding. Finally he announced: "We're going over to Phillips' shop and help him out." When they arrived, they were greeted with cold stares. The Phillips crew wouldn't even talk to them.

"We just went in and stood around for awhile and starting helping and picking up stuff," recalls Julian. "After awhile, they let us help. And we wound up working all night helping them."

The trip from Batesville to Springfield was about 200 miles on mostly two-lane roads. If driven at legal speed, the trip took almost four hours. Of course, Julian always drove the hauler and he never drove the speed limit. The record, Shaw remembers, was two hours and thirty-eight minutes.

Julian remembers the challenge: "When we pulled out of here on Friday going to Springfield, the school buses would be getting out. And you've got to stop behind these school buses. It's a two-lane road all the way up there and it's hilly and crooked. And we've got to fight the school buses all the way. It must be about sixty-four miles or so to the state line, and there's this ice cream joint right at the state line. If we got there in under and hour, we got to stop and get ice cream. If it took longer than an hour, we couldn't stop. Most times we got ice cream."

The team did not branch out further during the spring of 1977 because Mark was still in high school, completing his senior year. But school had become little more than a distraction for a teenager who already knew his life's work and was impatient to get on with it. On the night of his high-school graduation, Mark had a friend collect his diploma. He was busy breaking the track record in Springfield by half a second.

"He'd upped his grades enough when he was a senior that I told him if he made the honor roll, he wouldn't have to go to graduation," Julian says. "That's the only time he was ever on the honor roll."

With school behind him, Mark was ready to devote his life to racing.

Mark and Julian pause to watch Rusty Wallace head out to the track for his heat race before the thirty-lap feature. Most heat races and features were held at night.

"As soon as I got out of high school, I took a job at Larry Phillips' shop in Springfield," Mark recalls. "I had an apartment and I went to work every day and then met my team at the race track Friday night. It was a tremendous opportunity to learn from Larry over the summer. He'd throw a pile of material out on a bench and say, 'Build me this,' or 'Build me that,' and he'd leave. I didn't really know how to do it, and I'd have to figure it out. The more parts I made, the better I got at it. And pretty soon, I could make those parts for my car. I made upper control arms and lower control arms and different sheet-metal pieces. I became a better welder and a better fabricator."

Recalls Phillips: "Mark was a super good worker. The first job I gave him was gutting out an old Camaro body, scraping the tar out and cutting it up. It was hot work. But he just stayed right with her. We were kind of testing him. And if I'd been him, I would have gone home."

Mark's education as an asphalt racer grew that summer. Mark was racing at faster and faster tracks. And like all young drivers with the stamp of greatness, he had to find his limits by going over them. What were spinouts on dirt tracks became crashes on asphalt, sometimes with painful consequences.

At I-70 Speedway in Odessa, Missouri, in late May, Mark was injured for the first time. He chipped a bone in his shoulder in a crash on the high-banked asphalt track—one of the fastest in the midwest.

Five days later, back at Springfield, he won his sixth feature race of the season. Later in the summer, he was again hurt at Odessa.

"Odessa was a lot like Bristol—a big, fast and dangerous half-mile," Mark says. "Well, two guys in front of me tangled, and coming off the fourth corner, I spun trying to miss them. I went into the inside front stretch wall with my foot on the brake, pushing it as hard as I could."

His right foot came off the brake pedal and his big toe was dislocated when it hit part of the master cylinder.

"His toe. . . I can't even put anything in the shape of his toe," remembers Larry. "I don't know how in the world that toe ever got in that position. And he's sitting on the back of the stretcher asking me how bad the car was."

The emergency room doctor asked Mark: "How tough are you?"

"Well, I'm pretty darn tough."

The doctor took hold of the toe.

"I ain't *that* tough!" Mark said.

Travel to ever-more-distant tracks meant long hours on the road telling stories and cutting up. Julian snapped this photo of a relaxed and happy Mark outside West Plains, Missouri, on their way to the Friday night race at Springfield.

The doctor snapped his toe back into place. Mark let out a wail. He was on crutches for several days.

"I was in a lot of accidents in 1977," Mark recalls. "It was my reckless and accident-prone year. I was really fast, and I was on pavement, where you've got a lot more speed and you've got walls. I didn't have the knack for avoiding accidents. You just have to be in them to know how to miss them."

In June, Mark was profiled in *National Speed Sport News*. "I want to win the Daytona 500. . . and win it long before I'm twenty-five," he told writer J.J. O'Malley. The quote was widely repeated that year. Today, it still embarrasses Mark.

"I didn't create that and I didn't push that," he says. "It was created and it was pushed, but I really didn't do that. But, you know, at the rate we were going, it was possible. I still had seven years. If I had gone into a good Winston Cup car, I would have won a lot of races by the time I was twenty-five."

In 1977, Mark began running more and more races sanctioned by the American Speed Associa-

A pit stop at Winchester Speedway in 1977. Bill Davis, now a NASCAR Winston Cup car owner, is at left, next to Banjo Grimm. Julian is on the right side of the car. Dennis Martin and Larry Shaw handle the gas. Mark was leading the 400-lap race with 15 laps to go when his engine blew.

tion. The ASA series was the premier midwestern short-track series, and Mark had already raced against many of its top drivers, including Reffner and Schuler.

"All of a sudden, one day Rex Robbins called me," Mark says. "He is the president of ASA, and he said, "Hey, you've got 'Rookie of the Year' won. All you've got to do is run almost all of the races left on the schedule and you'll win.' That meant I had to go to the Minnesota State Fairgrounds, and to Winchester and Salem in Indiana, and to Cincinnati and Wausau, Michigan, and some other places."

The half-mile, high-banked track at Winchester, Indiana, is one of the oldest and fastest short tracks in the country. There, the ASA held a race named the Dri-Powr 400.

"It was a 400-lapper and it was the longest race I'd ever driven in my life," Mark says. He did not expect to win. He was just looking for a respectable finish. "I was leading with fifteen laps to go, and the engine blew up. That was a win we had in the bag that I could have never explained. I was that close—that close."

Several weeks later, at Salem Speedway, another high-banked track, Mark finished third. But the supreme test came on September 25 in Rockford, Illinois, and the 12th annual National Short Track Championship at Rockford Speedway. All of the best drivers were there: Reffner and Schuler and Dick Trickle, Mike Eddy, Dave Watson, Bob Strait and a young driver from St. Louis named Rusty Wallace. "We went up there the year before to look that race over and it scared the hell out of us just watching it," Shaw says.

Left: The National Short Track Championship at Rockford Speedway in Illinois, September 25, 1977. Never expecting to win, Mark took the lead on the 176th lap of the 200-lap race and was in front of Dave Roahrig by about three seconds when the checkered flag flew. In victory lane, Jackie Martin joined her son while track promoter Hugh Derry saluted the new national champ.

But Trickle, for one, knew that Mark had what it took to win races. "He had natural driving ability and desire. Desire is a big thing. You could tell with Rusty and him. They were go-getters and very serious about it and they decided they were going to make it."

Mark qualified second. "That in itself was pretty incredible," he says. At the start, Mark's goal was simply to survive. But he quickly discovered he could race with anyone. He spent the first half of the race trailing Reffner and Trickle. When Trickle crashed, and Reffner's car lost its clutch, Mark inherited the lead. He won by about three seconds.

"I won the race," he says today, disbelief still in his voice. "It was absolutely mind-boggling, and still is today. The fans went nuts."

Mark vividly remembers the victory lane ceremony. His orange driver's suit was about two sizes too big. "It was pathetic," he says. And the promoters made him put a large flower-covered wreath in the shape of a horseshoe around his shoulders. "They had this big old thing on me and I could hardly hold it up."

The victory capped off Mark's finest season yet. He was ASA Rookie of the Year, as well as track champion at Springfield and Fort Smith. The next goal was the ASA championship.

But in the pits at Rockford, the only thought was to celebrate. Julian brought out some Arkansas moonshine and taught Dick Trickle how to drink it. There was an art to drinking moonshine from a half-gallon jug, Julian explained. The object was to tip the jug nearly upside down and take several big gulps so that an air bubble shot upward. Teacher and pupil practiced, and the liquor took effect.

"Poor old Trickle would have liked to have died," Larry remembers. "I don't think he drove for a week."

"Yeah, we pretty near killed him," Julian agrees. "We had been racing together for four years, and we had never taken a drink connected with racing until then."

Larry says, "See, it was the race track's fault that we got that stuff out to begin with. They gave us this little bottle of champagne and we had that stuff gone in about five minutes. And we drank it instead of spraying it."

As darkness fell, Mark and Julian joked with each other before a race at Springfield Fairgrounds. Asked about details of the photo, Julian said "I don't have a clue. We were both so intense, especially me, I'm surprised someone caught us both laughing."

CHAPTER SIX

Above: The Batesville race shop is pictured on the first day the team began building the chassis Ed Howe sold Mark for the 1978 season. This engine was placed for position only and was replaced with a complete race engine. The trailer on the right carried tools and equipment to the races and had sides that could be removed in fifteen seconds.
Left: Mark's crew check the driveshaft and rear end for problems after a practice session.

"It was a heck of a recognition."

Mark's first meeting with car builder Ed Howe in the winter of 1977 had not been pleasant. Howe had mocked the team's carefully prepared Camaro. Mark had departed feeling humiliated. But Howe's attitude had changed.

Mark had first impressed Howe at New Smyrna. "All of a sudden they wanted to know, 'Who is this 110-pound kid driving this car?' I was eighteen then, but I looked like I was eleven, really," Mark recalls.

Later in the 1977 season, Mark had received a call from the Howe shop after finishing third in an ASA race at Owosso, Michigan.

"I had run the whole race trying to get under Bob Senneker and I couldn't get by," Mark says. "But Senneker was in one of Howe's house cars and I was quicker than him the whole race. And I'll always remember this. I got back to Arkansas and Herb Brannon called. He was the manager at Howe's. And instead of treating us like we were total idiots, like we were wasting their time, now they're nice to us. And he wanted to know what kind of setup we had under the car. And he'd say: 'Oh, by the way, we've got a better setup now. Just try these four springs and this weight and see if you don't like that even better.' "

"So that was pretty interesting. And that winter, after we won ASA Rookie of the Year, they called and said, 'Hey, we'll give you a free chassis for next year.' It wasn't much. It was probably $1,800. But it was a heck of a recognition. They wanted to make sure they had me in one of their race cars."

Howe had specific instructions about how to set up his house cars—the ones he raced out of his own shop. "We set up Howe's car exactly the way he said to set it up," Mark says. "We ran the car exactly the way he said to run it. And we didn't know anything else. We never went to a race track and changed a sway bar. Ed Howe said: 'Don't touch anything. Just change the tire stagger. Because the world is full of idiots and if you take my car and do what I tell you to do, and fix the tire stagger so it isn't pushing or loose, you'll win.'"

"And he was right."

Remembers Howe: "He was just a little snot-nosed kid. But I could tell he was eager and wanted to get the job done. You know, being so damn little—he could hardly see over the windshield— you must have something going for you. We had to block the seat way up high. It wasn't a normal position for the seat. And everything had to be changed so he could reach the pedals and see over the steering wheel."

But as Mark prepared to compete for the ASA championship, his Daytona dreams suddenly drew nearer. Ex-NASCAR driver Joe Frasson offered nineteen-year-old Mark his car for the 1978 Daytona 500. As brash and cocky as Mark and his father could be, they were cautious with this decision. They agreed that he needed more short track experience. They were on a fast track toward Daytona, but not that fast.

"I could go to Daytona and get all sorts of coverage, but what I really need is a sponsor and New Smyrna is more important to me," Mark told the *Springfield News and Leader* that winter. By 1978, Mark and his father were also feeling the pinch of the enormous cost of racing, and looking for sponsorship.

The finished car shows the influence that the weight-conscious Howe had on Mark's car construction. The bumpers are smaller and drilled for lightness and the tail section is wire mesh. Aluminum was used whenever possible.

Mark slipped into the car before one of its first races at New Smyrna. The yellow ignition coil was mounted on the dashboard to protect it from engine heat. A fire extinguisher was located behind Mark and activated by the red plunger on the cross tube.

"We shot the whole wad last year," he told the *News and Leader*. "We busted it wide open. We went out and bought anything we needed and hoped we got recognized."

And he did get recognized. In January 1978, Mark was profiled in *Stock Car Racing* magazine with a cover headline that read: "Youngster Wipes the Vets. Mark Martin Makes a Name For Himself."

But it didn't get him a sponsor.

"Let me tell you how sponsorship played out," Mark says today. "*There weren't any.* You couldn't get any. I never had a sponsor. Getting money to race cars, as far as I was concerned, was a total impossibility. What I did have, and the way I did it, was I got cheap help and volunteer help, I got a lot of free tires, a lot of free engines, a lot of free cars and a lot of free parts. Manufacturers' backing

is what I had and that's how I was able to make it. They all did it for product endorsement, and you ran their decals and endorsed their products."

1978 was a different kind of a year than 1977 had been in other ways, too.

"It was a long grind," Mark says. "It was tough because we knew we could run up front and we knew we could win. So we began to change from being excited every time we did well to expecting it. And it was a hard schedule pulling to all of these tracks from Arkansas." Now, the three-hour drive to Springfield seemed like a short trip when compared to the twelve-hour and fourteen-hour drives to tracks in Wisconsin and Minnesota.

"A typical weekend was Springfield on Friday night, and a little speedway up near Janesville, Wisconsin, on Saturday night, a little town over in Michigan on Sunday afternoon and then

Though it was still early in the season, a close look at the body showed the toll of competitive ASA racing. Lines of silver rivets along the nose and on either side of the door attested to replaced sheet metal.

sometimes back to Toledo, Ohio, on Sunday night. And then we'd be back on Monday morning to go to work," Julian says.

The team again opened the season at New Smyrna Speedway in Florida. This time, there was no crash. This time, he won the series. But he did not win any individual races. As it turned out, that set the tone for the season.

Although Mark led the ASA points most of the year, he did not win a race until the fifteenth event of the season—the Redbud 300 on August 19 at Anderson Speedway in Indiana. It was his first ASA race victory. It was a long time coming. But it was dramatic.

Two hundred and forty laps into the 300-lap race, Mark was on leader Dick Trickle's bumper as they sped around the tiny quarter-mile asphalt oval. But the handling on his car was deteriorating. Then Trickle began waving towards Mark's right rear tire. It was going down. A few laps later, with fifty to go, oil on the track brought out the yellow flag. Mark needed to pit. But on a quarter-mile track, even during a yellow flag, the risk was going a lap down. Julian made the decision. He ordered Mark to the pits.

Mark's sensational win in the Redbud 300 was made possible by a quick pit stop under caution. Julian's gamble to change only right-side tires got Mark out of the pits ahead of the pace car and kept him on the lead lap.

The crew frantically changed the tire. They had Mark back on the track in less than fourteen seconds. He was still on the lead lap. In the grandstands, more than 8,000 fans roared their approval.

Mark was third, trailing Trickle and Mike Eddy. When the green flag appeared, he passed Eddy. And for the next twenty-five laps, he battled Trickle through every turn before taking the lead on lap 286. A newspaper story described it this way: "A near-capacity crowd of 8,229 literally stormed the track gates as the nineteen-year-old charger rolled to a stop following the immensely popular victory—a triumph that capped a cliff-hanger race that saw Martin take the lead with only fourteen laps remaining after a pitched battle with Dick Trickle . . . ."

"My crew won the race for me," Mark said afterwards. "I couldn't believe how fast they got me out."

Now that he was an ASA regular, Mark followed the lead of many regulars and began racing in events sanctioned by the Wisconsin-based ARTGO stock-car racing series. His races in Springfield became few and far between. And he was missed. The word in Springfield and Fort Smith was that Mark didn't want to race against Phillips, who was once again dominating at both tracks. That wasn't the reason, Mark told Kirby Arnold of the *News and Leader*.

"I'm building my career," he said, "and I've got to race at places that will build my career. Nothing against Springfield or Fort Smith, but you don't get to Daytona from those places. I've got to move on."

At the National Short Track Championship that year, the team's effort to repeat the magic of 1977 dissolved into confused disappointment. Trickle beat Mark by six seconds after passing him rather easily on the 128th lap of the 250-lap race. Trickle had pitted early in the race to repair body damage, and Mark and his team seemed certain that Trickle was a lap down. Mark barely contested Trickle's pass. "I figured he was way back," Mark said after the race.

Still, Mark had a commanding lead in the ASA series. And at the October 22 ASA season finale at Queen City Speedway in Ohio, all Mark needed was a relatively low finish to clinch his first ASA title.

Instead, he won. The key to the victory was another fast pit stop. With only thirty-one of three hundred laps to go, Mark ducked into the pits and took on fresh tires. Then he charged through the

Mark could easily have coasted to the 1978 ASA Championship during the Buckeye 400 at the Queen City Speedway in Ohio. Instead he blitzed the field after a final tire change and took the victory, his second of the year.

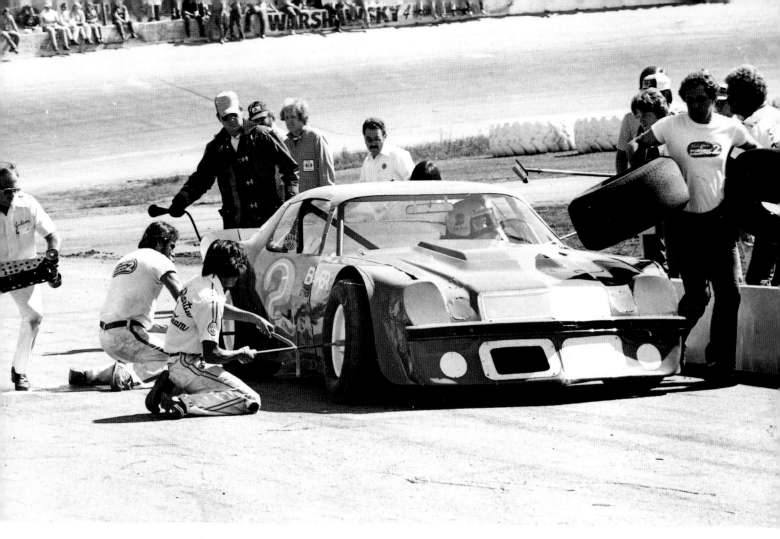

Teamwork played a big part in Mark's winning the championship. Pit stops, like this one during the Queen City 300, were fast, accurate and strategic. Mark pitted for tires in second place, rejoined in last place and within twenty laps passed the entire field to take the lead and the win.

pack, finally passing leader John Anderson with only eleven laps to go. At nineteen, Mark was the youngest ASA champion ever.

"A Mark Martin comes along only once in every ten years or so. He's that good," ASA President Rex Robbins said. "When you live in Batesville, Arkansas, and you make every race, you are truly a dedicated person. They have never wavered from their goal. I have had some of our best drivers tell me that in a year or two he'll really be a terror."

But Robbins also saw room for improvement. "Mark lacks a little experience," he said. "He lacks track savvy."

Mac DeMere, now a senior editor at *Motor Trend* magazine, was a young sportswriter with *The Clarion-Ledger* in Jackson, Mississippi, that year, and among his beats was Jackson International Speedway. Mark raced in Jackson because Julian's sister, Marilyn Hamlett, lived there. He could relax when he raced in Jackson.

When DeMere first saw Mark in the spring of 1978, the teenager looked almost comically out of place. He was small and so young looking. "Bewildered" was the word DeMere used, adding that Martin looked like "...at best, a first-year mini-stock driver."

Now he was different.

"His face was tanned, weathered and beginning to show wrinkle lines from a full summer spent on hot race tracks," DeMere wrote. "He laughed easily with an attractive girl while a crew member taped asbestos to his racing shoes to protect him from cockpit heat. Now, he looked at least a couple of years older than his actual nineteen years and acted like a confident champion."

Both of Mark's victories in 1978 had been come-from-behind wins that ignited the fans and made him one of the most popular young stock car racers in the midwest.

"Everybody just loves to see this fuzzy-faced kid whipping all the top dogs," Marilyn Hamlett told DeMere. "It's as American as apple pie."

But even as she spoke these words, this phase of Mark's career was over. With his championship came the expectation of success. No longer was he the under-aged underdog. The storybook triumphs by an overachieving youngster were now in the scrapbooks his mother religiously kept. From now on, Mark would be expected to win. He was comfortable with that. But it was a new feeling.

Change had also come to the Mark Martin Racing Team. At the end of the season, Larry Shaw resigned. He had a wife and two sons. And he was burned out. He took a job with Ray Baker, the engine builder who was supplying Mark's engines, and moved to Grand Rapids, Michigan, where Baker was located.

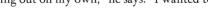

"Julian, Mark, and myself, we probably were about the closest of any three people," says Larry. "And that was probably what hurt us. We were around each other all the time. We didn't do nothing else. We didn't go to the lake, didn't go to the movies, we didn't do nothing but work on that race car all the time.

"If we had been split up a little bit, I'm going to say I would have been right there with Mark all the way up. But at times we just got on each other's nerves because we were around each other eighteen hours a day."

Father and son were increasingly at odds, as well. Julian recalls that "there were a lot of times after we got started that I thought 'What have I got set in motion here? This damn deal will never stop. And I guess I never wanted it to. We were so determined to excel and couldn't accept anything but perfection. That made it pretty goddamn hard on us a lot of the time."

It became clear to Mark that he had outgrown the family-run team. "I was very interested in getting out on my own," he says. "I wanted to be my own man."

Above: In the afternoon at Fairgrounds, Mark and Rusty Wallace talked about how they had run in the race. "Rusty and I spent a lot of time together", Mark says now. "We've raced together since 1977 and never had a problem. We've had one or two accidents together, but we've never had a problem." **Left:** By the end of 1978, tensions between Mark and Julian had increased. Mark wanted his independence to run his own team. "A lot of seventeen of or eighteen-year-olds have to have a burning desire to be in that situation," Mark says. "They're on their own and not living under the shadow of their parents."

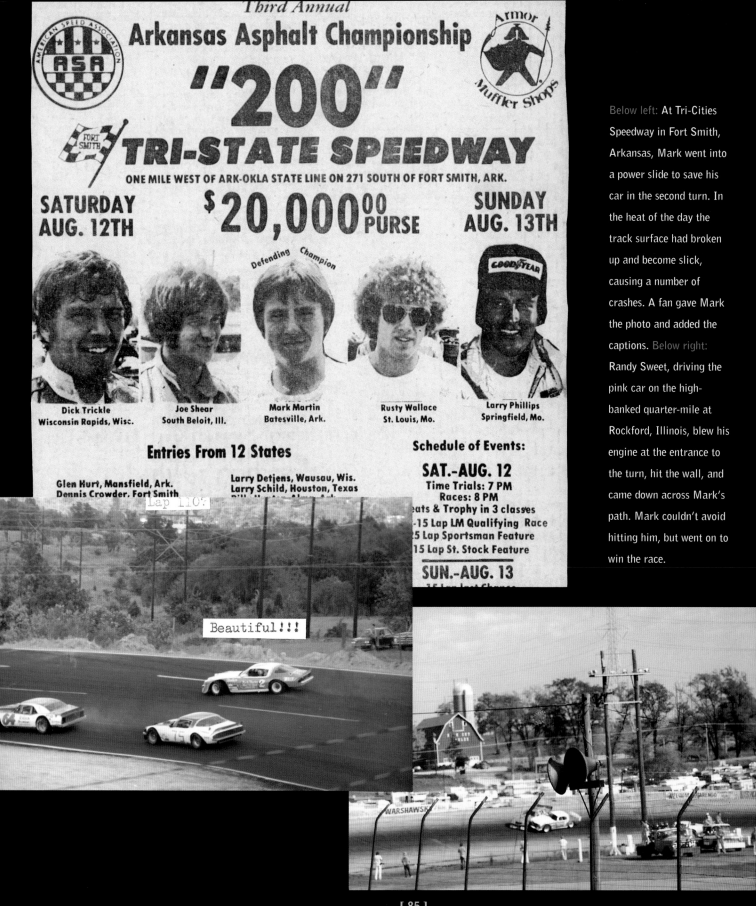

Third Annual

Arkansas Asphalt Championship

ASA — AMERICAN SPEED ASSOCIATION

Armor Muffler Shops

"200"

FORT SMITH TRI-STATE SPEEDWAY

ONE MILE WEST OF ARK-OKLA STATE LINE ON 271 SOUTH OF FORT SMITH, ARK.

SATURDAY AUG. 12TH

$20,000.00 PURSE

SUNDAY AUG. 13TH

Defending Champion

Dick Trickle
Wisconsin Rapids, Wisc.

Joe Shear
South Beloit, Ill.

Mark Martin
Batesville, Ark.

Rusty Wallace
St. Louis, Mo.

Larry Phillips
Springfield, Mo.

Entries From 12 States

Glen Hurt, Mansfield, Ark.
Dennis Crowder, Fort Smith

Larry Detjens, Wausau, Wis.
Larry Schild, Houston, Texas

Schedule of Events:

SAT.-AUG. 12
Time Trials: 7 PM
Races: 8 PM
Heats & Trophy in 3 classes
-15 Lap LM Qualifying Race
25 Lap Sportsman Feature
15 Lap St. Stock Feature

SUN.-AUG. 13

Lap 110:

Beautiful!!!

WARSHAWSK...

Below left: **At Tri-Cities Speedway in Fort Smith, Arkansas, Mark went into a power slide to save his car in the second turn. In the heat of the day the track surface had broken up and become slick, causing a number of crashes. A fan gave Mark the photo and added the captions.** Below right: **Randy Sweet, driving the pink car on the high-banked quarter-mile at Rockford, Illinois, blew his engine at the entrance to the turn, hit the wall, and came down across Mark's path. Mark couldn't avoid hitting him, but went on to win the race.**

CHAPTER SEVEN

"He was a visionary."

Above: In qualifying, the Martin team went to great lengths to set new track records. First they would wax the car, then dust baby powder on it. Next they would spray the sides of the tires and wheels with silicone and spray the entire underside of the car. These steps helped reduce the car's wind resistance.

Left: Rennie Wilbanks wrapped Mark's right foot with silver duct tape to insulate it from the engine heat that came into the footwell area. This was a standard part of their preparation for long races.

Each February at Daytona during Speedweeks, parts suppliers, car builders, and racing merchants flock to *Circle Track* magazine's annual trade show. A lot of bartering takes place as short-track racers from around the country—in Florida for the World Series at New Smyrna—try to make deals for parts, and the manufacturers try to figure out who are the hottest prospects. As the ASA champion, Mark had had a strong bargaining position. But on the eve of the 1979 season, he also thought the show might hold the key to his independence.

"I was the reigning ASA champion at a freshly turned twenty years old, and I was working deals with all the manufacturers for free tires, free shocks, and other free parts," Mark recalls. "And I ran across Ray Dillon, a parts man who had a place in North Liberty, Indiana. And I saw he had springs, but I didn't care about springs yet. I didn't change springs anyway. But he had trailers. And so I said, 'How about a deal on a free trailer?'

"And so he says, 'I'll tell you what I'll do. I'll do you a deal on a free trailer, and springs, and if you want, I'll give you a shop to work out of. I've got a three-bedroom house and I'll rent it to you for $150 a month.' So I went home, packed my stuff and moved to Indiana."

Dillon had seen Mark race a year earlier at New Smyrna. "He was extremely young," Dillon recalls. "But they came in there with a very professional-looking set-up. The crew all had uniforms. The truck and trailer was all lettered up. And he was competitive."

Dillon had a dream. He wanted to build a race car "that was going to whip the world." With Mark, he saw a way to fulfill it.

Mark says: "He was a visionary. His plan was that he was going to grab me, get me up to North Liberty and get me in there with him. And then after we got rolling, he was going to build a race car. He was going to go up against Ed Howe. I never dreamed what he had in mind."

Dillon says, "The idea of building a super chassis had been in my mind for several years. But at that time, it didn't include Mark. I was going to be the driver. I had been racing the local tracks around here for seven or eight years.' Well, we got to talking at the trade show about how tough it was to commute from Arkansas to the ASA races, which were primarily in my backyard at the time. So I got this instant idea. I said, 'Well, Mark, why don't I just take a year off from racing, and you bring all your stuff and move into my garage, help me promote my Cobra Coil springs and my trailers, bring your Howe chassis and race out of my building, and I'll help you. And it's all free.'

"The next thing he said was, 'Well, is there a house for rent around there?' And I said, 'Yeah, there just happens to be one right on the same property that is going to be vacant.' And I shot him a rent figure. Our whole initial meeting — discussing the direction we wanted to go in life, my offer, shaking hands — took fifteen minutes."

When Mark arrived in North Liberty, he found that Dillon didn't have much.

He says: "The shop was more like a pole barn, where you put poles up and siding on it and a roof. There was no insulation, and the winters are horrid there. And there was no heat. Of course, that didn't bother me at all. We had this space heater that looks like a torpedo, blowing around those fumes from the diesel fuel. But it didn't bother me. I was happy. Me and my boys. I had two or three full-time employees and we all lived in the house. I paid the rent. I paid my employees $100 a week and I didn't pay myself anything, just whatever I had to have.

"And we set up shop there, and Dillon's shop was next door. Anything he made, hand-made parts, I got for free. And anything he had to buy, I paid what he paid. And of course, he bought it cheap, because he had a parts place."

Mark's right-hand man, and his crew chief, in 1979, would be Bill "Banjo" Grimm, who had joined the team in 1977. Banjo, now a veteran NASCAR Winston Cup crewman, had hooked up with Mark after working for him during a race in Cincinnati.

"Riding back, we said, 'Okay, Banjo, where do you want us to drop you off?' He wouldn't say," Mark recalls. "He didn't want to go home. So he went home with me. And he lived in my house and wore my clothes and drove my car and dated my girlfriend once. I had to whup him over that. But we were like family for years."

Recalls Banjo: "It was like, 'If it's all right with you, I'll just go back to Arkansas.' We got there in the middle of

the night and he put me up in a room. I woke up the next day and somebody was picking my clothes up. Turns out it was the maid they had. We walked outside and they had a beautiful home on a bluff overlooking Batesville and an in-ground pool. I had never seen any of this kind of stuff. It was just amazing."

Working out of North Liberty, Mark started 1979 as he had ended 1978—with a victory. He won a 100-lap ASA race on the high banks at Winchester. He didn't win in ASA again until September 3 at St. Paul, Minnesota, but he won other races and ran consistently well. By the time he won the World Cup 400 at I-70 Speedway in Odessa, Missouri, on a hot Sunday afternoon in October, Mark had all but clinched his second straight ASA championship. He locked it up the last weekend of October in Cincinnati, finishing third in the ASA season finale.

Midwestern races in the early spring can be chilly affairs, and one of Mark's team members decided that it was more important to keep the tires warm than himself. Tires need to be hot to give maximum cornering grip.

But in 1979, Mark's Daytona dream seemed more elusive than ever. In February, in addition to meeting Dillon, Mark had learned some of NASCAR racing's harsh realities.

"That's when I began to wonder if I'd ever make it," he told interviewers in late 1979. "It's really tough and it costs so much to run there. I can't do it now because of the cost. I've talked to a few companies about sponsoring me, but they aren't that interested in advertising with a race car. I used to have (long-range) goals, but most of them have mellowed out. There's no way in hell of getting into NASCAR on less than a quarter of a million dollars. I've seen drivers try and come back not because they couldn't drive, but because they couldn't afford it."

Still, 1979 was a year of freedom and self-discovery for Mark.

"We were a hell of a team," Mark says. "And I was the happiest man on earth. We were kids who worked eighteen hours a day, seven days a week, doing nothing but racing. Trickle told the media that we were going to burn out. We set a new standard for racing in ASA because of hard work and preparation. Everyone else was racing and partying all the time and we were almost too young to party."

During a break in the action at the Snowball Derby in Pensacola, Florida, Mark talked with Mike Alexander (right) and another racer. "Mike was a tremendous competitor who wound up suffering a head injury in a crash during that race," Mark remembers.

Trickle remembers being impressed by Mark's detailed preparation of his cars. "They were buffed and shined. Even the aluminum was polished on the interior—*they actually polished the aluminum*. His cars were immaculate. I'd be racing somewhere on a Thursday night and travel all night and get to a track with a bunch of things to do and there's Mark, sitting on his fender, buffed, polished, and ready to go. And he taught me one thing. One of the ingredients to winning races is being ready. They always were."

Says Banjo: "When we unloaded at a race track, people were just in awe of us. It was because we worked so hard. We just didn't leave any stone unturned. We worked our guts out night and day. It was common for us to be out in the shop at two, three, four in the morning, with snow blowing in under the doors and through the windows."

"My dad still came and helped," Mark says. "And he came to most of the races. We were on much better terms. I had my independence and he was doing his thing and things were okay. And he still helped me financially, too. I paid all the bills, but from time to time he gave me something or bought me something."

Dillon, meanwhile, built a rough prototype chassis and put a body on it. In August, Mark ran the experimental car in a race in Michigan. The car was different — it had coil-over shocks, which meant that the shock absorber was inside the coil spring instead of being mounted separately. This allowed the spring and shock to work almost as a single unit. And that improved handling, which made the car faster. Coil-over shocks were not unique; several other ASA racers used them. But they were not predominant, either.

"We ran the car and it didn't run worse than my car," Mark recalls. "It was a very crude car. Dillon's fabricating was not polished at all. But we ran pretty good."

After the race, and after a few beers, Dillon and Mark began perfecting Dillon's experiment. They called the new chassis the Mark II.

"We made a pact," Mark says. "And I told him, 'We're not building this on the floor. You've gotta get me a nice jig.'"

Recalls Dillon: "It was going to be, shall we say, Indy car technology adapted to a stock car, with coil-over shocks and rack-and-pinion steering. One of the main advantages is that it's a lot lighter. And another thing we were going to do is build our own front clip. Most of the cars at that time, from the fire wall back, were made out of tubing, but still utilized a stock front clip. There were two reasons for building our own front clip. One is that it would be lighter and, secondly, we could more easily alter the geometry.

After winning the ASA season-opening Champion Motor Home 100 on the high banks of Winchester Speedway in Indiana, Mark posed with the trophy girl. It was the first of three victories in that championship season.

"And I called the company we bought steel from and ordered a ground piece of plate three inches thick, six feet wide, and fifteen feet long, for a fee of $5,000, which in 1979 was a hell of a lot of money. But it was our surface plate. And Mark and I started locating the pivot points where we wanted them. And we did all of this with a square, a level, string, and a tape measure."

"Our goal was to have a car done to run in the Snowball Derby the first weekend in December at Pensacola, Florida. And we did that. It was probably the lightest stock car that had ever been built. They had a weight rule. We had to weigh 2,800 pounds. And our biggest problem was we couldn't find enough lead to get the car heavy enough."

Mark didn't win in Pensacola, but the Mark II car showed tremendous potential. "It was Ray's brainchild," Mark recalls. "All I did was keep it grounded and make sure all this stuff was practical and was repeatable."

As the 1980 season progressed, however, Mark was handicapped by another problem: tires. He was a loyal Firestone user, but the Firestones had slipped in performance. "I worked and worked

At the Milwaukee Mile in May, Mark's team gave him a state-of-the-art pit stop, ASA-style. Jim Hamlett carries a right front tire back over the wall (above) while Bruce Baker cleans the front grille.

and worked and worked with them in late 1979 and into the 1980 season, but I was slow. I couldn't run fast," Mark says.

Tires weren't a problem in the season opener at Cincinnati. He set a track record and won the race. But by May, as the series headed to Milwaukee, Mark was struggling.

"I was beat at Milwaukee," he recalls. "I couldn't do it anymore with the Firestones. I'd taken about $800 cash with me, which I had borrowed from my Dad, and I was prepared to buy Goodyear tires. The night before the track opened, I went to bed in the motel room. When I woke up in the morning, I turned over and noticed that my door was slightly open. And I looked on the dresser, and my wallet was still there."

"So I got up, took a shower, got dressed and went to McDonald's to get some breakfast. I pulled my wallet out. It was empty. I didn't have a dime. I gave them the food back and went to the track. And I struggled throughout the whole practice session. I was slow. I knew what loyalty was. And I knew I was going to hurt myself with Firestone. But I couldn't do it anymore. I walked up to the Goodyear truck and had them mount four Goodyear tires. They let me have them on credit. I had never driven on a Goodyear tire before in my life. I never had a chance to practice with them. Before I went out, I changed all the springs and shocks and put everything back at a starting point. And I just went out cold turkey and qualified. And I set a track record and won the pole."

He won the 150-lap race as well, and it was another classic come-from-behind victory for 'The Kid.' Mark had been battling Bob Strait for the lead when a botched pit stop sent him back to fifteenth. Mark then "put on one of the most exciting charges at State Fair Park in recent years," *The Milwaukee Journal* reported. It kept a crowd of more than 15,000 "constantly on its feet cheering."

Mark cut through the field. Each time he passed a car, he coached himself: "Go. Go get the next one." With twenty-five laps to go, Mark passed Alan Kulwicki and moved into 4th place. He passed Strait for 3rd with 21 to go, and 5 laps later passed Bob Senneker for 2nd. And with 14 laps to go, going into the first turn, Mark dove below leader Dick Trickle and took the lead, sending the crowd to its feet once more."

With Goodyear tires on the Mark II chassis, Mark now had the most potent race car of his ca-

reer. And he proved it in the next ASA race, winning on the high banks at Winchester, and then finishing second in the next three races. The Mark II was an unqualified success.

"It almost became a rule that you had to have one to be competitive," says Dillon. "Within a couple of years, if they started forty cars, I think about thirty-six of them were mine. We went from three employees to twenty-seven.

"But we couldn't build cars as fast as people wanted them. And what really revolutionized the thing was I came up with a conversion kit. You could buy from me the lower A-frames, the coil-over shocks, the mounting brackets and a blueprint and you could convert your Howe car into a Mark II. I guess when I knew we were on the right track is when Ed Howe himself called me and bought fifty conversion kits."

Mark says: "It was revolutionary in the sport. They had fifteen ASA races in 1980. And I sat on the pole eleven times and won five and ran second in five. You couldn't lose a championship running like that. It forced Trickle to buy one. It forced Rusty Wallace to buy one. It forced everybody I raced against to go to Dillon's and buy a car. It revolutionized short-track racing. And I'm going to tell you—it was Ray Dillon. I had my part in manipulating it, but he had the idea. He was the guy standing down there at the trade show who said, 'I'm going to get this kid up there and I'm going to go head-to-head with Ed Howe.' And he did, and he about broke Ed Howe's back."

"I think it was of benefit to us," Howe says today. "We were resisting the trend to go to lighter cars and probably that was the spur of getting us to move."

Since Mark was chiefly interested in racing the car, and Dillon was interested in selling them—lots of them—a slight conflict arose.

"There were a lot of lookers," Dillon says. "Mark tried to keep them away. But I always brought people over to show it to them. Obviously, I wanted to sell cars. And he wanted to keep it a secret. One time, this guy had the trunk lid open and had his head stuck clear in there, looking at the rear suspension. And Banjo slammed the trunk lid on the guy's head. So I had to explain to Banjo that in terms of the overall success of what we were trying to do, we didn't want to be slamming hoods on peoples' heads."

HELP FOR A WINNER — Mark Martin, who drove with a broken ankle, was helped from his car after winning the American Speed Association stock car 15 Fair Park Thursday in a Trickle.

CHAPTER EIGHT

"We were both on crutches."

On July 6, 1980, Mark was at the Capital Super Speedway near Madison, Wisconsin, for an ARTGO race.

"They had inverted the field, so I had to come through the pack," Mark recalls. "I got my nose underneath Jim Sauter, and he pinched me down to the bottom of the track. Rather than turn him around, I tried to get out of there. You didn't race rough in ARTGO. And I spun."

Bob Strait slammed into the driver's side of Mark's car. Strait's nose penetrated in the vicinity of Mark's lower legs and feet.

"When Strait hit me, I knew I was busted up," Mark says. "There was a pretty good little bit of pain. They flew me out of there in a military helicopter."

In Madison General Hospital, doctors found that Mark had four broken bones in his left foot. His left leg was broken, and so was his right ankle.

"My doctor told me I wouldn't race again that year," Mark says. "I told him, 'I'll race again in four weeks.' This doctor was (Olympic speed skater) Eric Heiden's father, so he somewhat understood what I was saying."

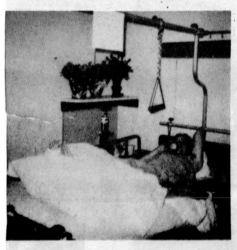

MARTIN INJURED AT CAPITAL

Mark Martin sustained a broken left ankle (in five places), a broken left leg and a broken right ankle in his accident at the Pepsi 100 at Capital Super Speedway Sunday afternoon. Mark is at Madison General Hospital and is expected to be released Thursday when he will return to Arkansas to recuperate. His mailing address is 66818 S.R. 23, North Liberty, IN 46554, which will be forwarded to him until he returns to the shop.

Top left: Two of the biggest stars in the ASA series, Mark and veteran Bob Senneker, roll away at Winchester. **Above:** On July 6, 1980 Mark sustained his first serious racing injury when his car was hit on the driver's side by Bob Strait during an ARTGO race.

Benny Sieu
at State
ith Dick

Four days after the crash, Mark was released from the hospital and went home to Batesville with casts on both legs. The immediate challenge was another ASA race in LaCrosse, Wisconsin, on July 20. Mark knew he couldn't drive. Before his crash, Mark had been negotiating with NASCAR Winston Cup star Darrell Waltrip to drive another Dillon car in some ASA races later that season. After his crash, Mark called Waltrip, who agreed to drive Mark's car in Wisconsin.

Julian agreed to come help, and they left at night, with Julian driving a Chevy Suburban and Mark on a mattress in the back, elevating his shattered feet. Just before daybreak, Julian stopped for gas in Bloomington, Illinois. Mark was sleeping.

Julian says: "I went around the side of this service station to get a soft drink. And I heard something. It sounded like the ring of a volleyball when you hit it real hard with your fist. And about the third ring, I looked up just in time to see a wheel coming at me. Some guy had been coming down the road pulling a boat trailer and the whole damn wheel came off. And every time

After winning the Memorial 300 at Winchester, Mark was flanked by two trophy girls. Behind Mark is his former brother-in-law, David Lovendahl on the left, and Banjo Grimm on the right. Both men are involved in NASCAR racing today.

After a practice session at Milwaukee, Mark climbed from the car. The fast-moving crew has already jacked the car and started working on the right side.

it hit the ground, it made that ringing sound. I saw it just in time to throw my hand down, and it broke my little finger. It hit me in the side of the leg and broke my knee out of its socket and my leg went out and naturally I was not feeling real good. So they called an ambulance and they hauled me down to the hospital."

Sometime later, Mark awoke. "I was laying there in the back, and I finally got tired of waiting," he recalls. "It seemed like I'd been there forever. I finally crawled to the door and opened it and shouted, 'Y'all seen my dad?'

"Someone said, 'Yeah, they took him to the hospital.'"

Julian says, "The doctors decided the knee wasn't broken, so they got it back in the socket and turned me loose. And I'm hurtin' as bad as I ever hurt in my life. I held onto the wall and handwalked my way out of the hospital, got a cab and went back to the station. When I got there, Mark was awake—and madder than a damn snake."

Julian began driving, but he was in so much pain, Mark insisted on taking over.

"My left foot and ankle was broken in four places, and it would throb if blood went to it," Mark says. "So I had had my left foot up on the dash."

On they went up the highway. In Wisconsin, Julian went to another hospital and had a cast put on his aching leg.

"When we checked into the motel, I had all these pillows to elevate my leg in the car," Mark says. "We're both on crutches, with pillows hanging out of our mouths and suitcases on our fingers.

Mark and Dick Trickle run side-by-side at Wisconsin International Raceway. Julian remembers that Trickle had predicted that the intense Martin team would burn itself out and that he would win the championship.

I mean, you talk about pitiful. . . ."

Julian recalls, "When we pulled into the race track, Mark was in a wheelchair, with casts on both feet. And I in a cast and on crutches. We were a sorry pair. People in the pits were laughing at us and making a lot of remarks.

"One of my jobs was tire stagger. The NASCAR guys back then didn't fool with tire stagger. So I was doing the tires, and I couldn't keep up with the crutches. So I flung them away and started walking on the damn cast. And I'm hot and sweating and my face is blood red, and Waltrip shows up. And he's all spiffy, you know. And he looks at me and says, 'What are you doing?' And he thought it was ridiculous that I was spending all that time on the tires. He said, 'What you need to do is cool down.' "

"Then Mark came rolling up in his wheelchair and he was hyper as hell. And he immediately jumps all over Waltrip. He said, 'This is my car, and I know the car is capable of winning. I want this car to sit on the pole and win the race.' "

"Waltrip looked at him and said, 'Yes, sir.' " And that's exactly what he did.

"He had to race hard to win the race," Mark recalls. "He had to outduel Trickle. But he was just so happy to win. He was used to coming in and getting junk to drive."

Waltrip says, "I was a little skeptical about how we were going to do. Mark was not skeptical at all. He was very positive about how we were going to do. He sat in that little wheelchair with his leg stuck up in the air and he orchestrated everything. And he sent me on my way."

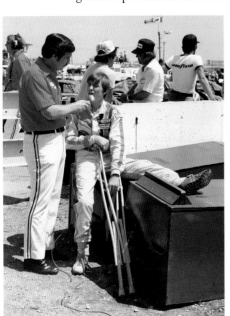

"I could barely get in the car. You know how small he is and how big I am. And they had compensated for that a little bit, but not near enough. So I wasn't very comfortable. But the car was killer fast. But it was nip and tuck to win the race. We raced Dick Trickle tooth and nail. We finally did beat him at the end. I remember being worn out after the race because I didn't fit in the car well. It was a good deal for both of us. I needed to win a race and he needed somebody to do it."

During the race, Waltrip didn't realize he had a fast pit crew.

"When we got through and dropped the jack, he just sat there," recalls Julian. "Mark and I both were hollering, 'Go! Go! Go!' He came on the radio afterwards and said, 'I couldn't believe you were finished.' "

Martin, Hand Clutching, Beats ASA Aces, Rain at Milwaukee

MILWAUKEE — Mark Martin, still recuperating from month-old racing injuries including virtually no use of his left leg, won a sensational duel with Dick Trickle that went to the wire in the "Ams/Oil Badgerland 150" for American Speed Association (ASA) National Circuit of Champions Series late models Thursday at State Fair Park Speedway.

BAD WEATHER

But the entire afternoon was a running battle with rain, high linds, tornado warnings and a tight Wisconsin State Fair schedule that made the entire event a candidate for Ripley's "Believe It Or Not."

Due to a wet track it was decided to scrub time trials and give the entire 57-car field a shot at $29,900 purse.

At 3:40 p.m., 54 cars took the green flag following an abbreviated practice session.

The race lined up according to ASA point standings plus a blind draw, resulting in point leader Martin taking the pole, sided by Bob Senneker and followed by Mike Eddy, Trickle, Bob Strait, Don Gregory and a pack including Darrell Waltrip in the experimental, vee-six Baker Buick; Rusty Wallace, winner of three straight USAC races at the track and a virtual who's - who of midwest stock car racing.

Those brave enough to open their eyes after the first lap saw a tremendously competitive race developing, with Martin leading

the first five circuits, E. taking over to lap 24, Trickle then heading a 15- lead group for a single Senneker took charge at 26-lap mark and maintai the lead for a comparat ly long 20 laps.

Despite 45 cars still on track, the first caution n't appear until lap 38 that was for cleanup of Je Wood's blown engine.

TRICKLE LEADS

Trickle took the lead w the green flag appeared lap 46 but he was hounde a group including Senne Eddy, Butch and M Miller, Dave Watson, M tin and Jim Sauter, who been forced to dash into pits for six seconds on four to repair a loose h pin. Waltrip parked Buick for good with tra (Turn to Page 38)

Left: Four weeks after breaking his right foot and his left foot and ankle in four places, Mark was interviewed by the track announcer at Milwaukee. His left leg was elevated to improve circulation.

Above: After the Milwaukee race, pain and fatigue were etched on Mark's face as his crew lifted him from the car. At times during the race the pain was so intense, Mark radioed to the pit that he couldn't do it anymore. "You <u>have</u> to do it!" Julian told him.

As Mark slowly healed, he worried about his future. He worried about money. He worried that his injury might hurt his future. Three weeks after his crash, Mark returned to Dr. Heiden, who cut the cast off. He told Mark he would go faster without it.

"He told me if I wrecked I would break it again," Mark recalls. "But it was real important for me to win the championship. Because it was going to be the last year I ran for the championship. I was going to go NASCAR fortune hunting. The very first race back was an ASA race in Milwaukee. I hadn't had to miss an ASA race. But we had to put a hand clutch in the car because I couldn't push the clutch pedal with my left foot. My right foot was just fractured and I could still use it for the gas and the brakes."

Coming in The
"Back Door"

Mark! you don't
have to...

Mark set a track record on the Milwaukee mile. And then he won the race, using his hand clutch. But he was so exhausted after taking the checkered flag, he drove into the pits the wrong way. His face was a mask of pain and exhaustion as he was helped out of his car. Behind him, Banjo Grimm was delirious with joy and relief.

Banjo says, "He had won the race, and his legs were bleeding through the casts. I mean it was just... wow. And that victory kept him going in the championship drive. He was still leading the points, and he just never let up."

Over his years of racing, the one racer Mark always seemed to encounter everywhere he went was Rusty Wallace. They had first met at Winchester in the mid-1970s when Rusty arrived with a brand-new red Firebird that impressed Mark so much, he introduced himself.

"He was always so young-looking," recalls Wallace. "They called him 'The Kid' for a long time. Then his career really took off. He started paying a lot of attention to the cars. He worked real hard on shocks and springs and he just mowed down the competition for a long, long time."

They became friends, at least as racers become friends.

"Once I went to Jackson, Mississippi, to race," Rusty recalls. "Mark wasn't racing that weekend, so he got in my hauler and we went down to Jackson. I got in the race, and my old car is running pretty good, and Mark was spotting for me."

"Well, the damn thing blew an engine. And it blew so bad, it blew the starter off and a whole bunch of other stuff and the car went flying off the track in the air and on fire. The fire was so bad it caught all the grass on fire. That was a pretty spectacular sight. And Mark said he was never going to spot again. Those were some really wild

After testing NASCAR veteran Bobby Allison's ASA car, Mark offered some suggestions on fine tuning the suspension. Mark helped Ray Dillon design the chassis Allison was driving. He was twenty-one. Car owner Ray Young (left) and Mark Miller listen in.

days. We were outlaws running everywhere in the country. And we were all running together."

1980 was Mark's finest season in ASA.

After his victory in Milwaukee, he set a track record at Indianapolis Raceway Park, finished second in Anderson, and then set track records in each of the final five events. He also won at Salem and Odessa.

"It was by far the most incredible year I've ever had," Mark says. "Two kids basically did all this. Banjo and I. Nobody told us what to do. Nobody made any motel reservations for us. Banjo and I and a couple of other guys who worked for us managed this whole program. We were twenty-one years old and we were doing it."

Even at that young age, Mark had no worlds left to conquer in ASA. "Maybe some people are satisfied to remain where they are and be king of the hill there," Julian commented. "Hell, everytime we became king of the hill we headed up to a higher hill."

And now, finally, that higher hill was NASCAR.

CHAPTER NINE

Mark's First G.N. Race 4-5-81 No. Wilkesboro N.C.

NASCAR®

PIT PERMIT 0

GOOD FOR ENTRY IN MOTOR PITS ONLY

NAME OF PERMIT HOLDER

NOT VALID FOR ENTRANCE WITHOUT ATTACHED STUB

No. 1068

GLOBE TICKET COMPANY 5260

"Better drill some holes in the floorboard."

Above: Mark's first Winston Cup pit pass from North Wilkesboro, dated 4-5-81 by Jackie.

Left: When Mark first raced in the sportsman class at Daytona in February 1981, his car encountered problems. NASCAR inspectors complained that the rocker panels were too wide and that the left side extra weight rail had holes. They demanded immediate changes.

With the success of 1980, Mark, Banjo and Ray Dillon embarked on a frenzy of building for 1981. They built an ASA car, an "outlaw" car for ARTGO and other races, a NASCAR Sportsman (now Busch Grand National) car, and a Winston Cup car.

Mark decided to compete in an ARCA race at Talladega, five Sportsman races on larger speedways and five Winston Cup short-track races. He became a part-time competitor in ASA and Midwest racing. His goal for Winston Cup debut was formidable: A pole or a victory. Or, at the very least, a top-five finish.

Dillon says, "Mark and I built a chassis together and we shipped it South to have a body installed. It never got worked on. So after about three months, Mark and I decided to jump in an airplane and go down there and see what was going on, and we found it sitting out behind the building covered with rust."

Mark found someone else to do the job, but Dillon remembers that it cost him at least $5,000 — "more than I was selling a total race car for."

Recalls Mark: "Ray probably had $20,000 to $25,000 invested in it at the time, which was horrendous for what we were used to."

The Ray Dillon chassis with a fresh Pontiac Ventura body rolls out of Will Cronkrite's shop in Fort Mill, South Carolina. Another body installer had delayed Mark and Dillon for three months before they reclaimed their chassis and took it to Cronkrite.

Mark finished thirteenth in his debut at Daytona International Speedway in the Sportsman race, but at Rockingham one week later, in only his second event, he won the pole for the Sportsman race with a lap of 144.125 miles per hour. His fun ended there. "We blew a right front tire and totaled the car," Mark says. "It was a throwaway. We killed it. And that killed Ray."

"I wasn't in a mood to spend that much money again," says Dillon. "But Mark was ready to go Winston Cup racing. So I compromised with him." Dillon built the chassis; Mark did the rest.

Mark Martin made his Winston Cup debut on April 3, 1981, at North Wilkesboro Speedway, NASCAR's oldest track. He recalls, "I was the senior person on our race team. And I was twenty-two years old. I qualified fifth. But we were still just as ignorant as pie. They started the race with the track wet. We started with the yellow and green flags together, and I was so nervous about that, I forgot to turn on the rear-end cooler pump. We had never run a rear-end pump before. I didn't think about turning it on. So the rear end burned up right away."

Mark completed 166 laps, but also lost a cylinder in the engine and was overwhelmed by the smoke from the burning rear end. When he dropped out of the race, he had to be pulled from the car. He was not discouraged. One week later, at Darlington Raceway, Mark won the outside pole position for the Sportsman race.

"I've got my car up to a respectable speed," Mark said that day. "Now I just want to get where I can race with those other guys up front and not be a hazard. I don't want anyone saying Mark Martin was a hazard on the track. That's why I'm here in the Sportsman race instead of the Rebel 500. I want to get some experience."

Above: During Speedweeks in February, Mark also raced in the World Series at New Smyrna in his ASA car. Fatigue shows on his face. The day began at 5 AM at Daytona and ended at New Smyrna at 1 AM. Dick Trickle is exiting the pit lane behind him.

Left: In his second race in the NASCAR Sportsman class (renamed the Busch Grand National Series) at Rockingham, Mark won the pole. He ran well before the right front tire blew and he crashed, totaling the team's new car.

Right: Mark qualified sixth for his second Winston Cup race at Nashville. In the final practice session his engine blew and he joined the crew in working on the car to get it ready for the race the next day.

Below: Unfortunately, a broken camshaft ended Mark's Nashville race on the second lap. When it became clear that he couldn't rejoin the race he went out to watch and study how different cars' chassis worked in turns.

His second Winston Cup start came at Nashville on May 9. Once again, he was strong in qualifying, finishing sixth. He blew an engine in the last practice session, and personally dove under the hood to help change it. But in the race, Mark's camshaft broke on the second lap and he finished last in a 27-car field.

"I took my car home to Indiana and I cut it up," Mark says. "I cut up the chassis geometry and went all through it and changed it to be more like a Winston Cup car. I had no senior figure helping me. There was nobody from NASCAR country on my team. All of this was stuff I was figuring out for myself. Two months later, we took it back to Nashville. And I sat on the pole."

It was only his third Winston Cup start. Afterwards, Mark said, "When I started that race car this year, I had high hopes of doing one of two things. I wanted either to win a race or win a pole, because either one of them is a tremendous financial boost. It's just tremendous to really do one, considering the guys I'm competing against out there."

Even though the July 11 race was at night, it was a scorcher. After the final practice, Dale Inman, Richard Petty's crew chief, stopped by. "Better

Martin Pulls Surprise With 420 Pole Spot

BY GARY McCREDIE
Editor

NASHVILLE, Tenn. (July 10)—Mark Martin of North Liberty, Ind., who last year decided that Winston Cup Grand National racing would be the key to his success as a professional driver, tonight became the 11th driver this year to qualify for next February's prestigious Busch Clash for 1981 pole winners at Daytona International Speedway.

Driving a Pontiac built by Will Cronkrite of Ft. Mill, S.C., and sponsored by Ams/Oil, a synthetic lubricant, the 22-year-old, three-time American Speed Association Late Model champion won the pole for the Busch Nashville 420 at Nashville International Raceway. His time of 20.561 seconds—104.353 mph—around the 0.625-mile speedway was 1.41 seconds faster than that of Ricky Rudd of Chesapeake, Va., who will start the DiGard Gatorade Chevrolet on the outside front row.

"In the race tomorrow night, I just want to be a good strong competitor," remarked Martin. "Harry Hyde (who helped Martin and his crew set up the car) told me after the last practice session that I was four-tenths of a second faster than everybody. But it was like a dream come true. It was unbelievable.

"I told everybody it would be a good week for me here. I've rode my bad luck

(American Speed Association). All they did was put a Grand Prix body on it."

Rudd also noted that the car he brought to Nashville, a Monte Carlo, was built only recently and will be used this year on the circuit's shorter tracks.

"The car will be used for tracks like this and for the one-mile tracks," he said. "The crew just seemed to like the (Monte Carlo) body style, so they went ahead and built one."

Including this event, Martin has entered three Winston Cup races this year. He ran the spring event at North Wilkesboro, N.C. and the May Melling Tool 420 here but fell out of both races early with mechanical problems. He will run two more races this year, thus staying within the five-race maximum which will qualify him to run for the rookie of the year title in 1982.

Martin's car owner is Bud Reeder of Denver, Colo., whom he met through short-track racing. Like Martin, Reeder, an ex-short-track racer himself, and the rest of the crew are all novices on the GN trail.

"I feel lucky (to win the pole), because I know how competitive these guys are," said Martin. "I need to start preparing for it (the Busch Clash) right now. I can't believe I'm in it. I just can't believe it."

Qualifying third at 103.568 mph was Benny Parsons in the Melling Tool Ford Thunderbird, the winner of the May race here. Darrell Waltrip was fourth fastest at 103.563 in the Mountain Dew

Mark Martin is now the eleventh driver eligible for the Busch Clash.

Chevrolet, 103.348 mph; defending Busch Nashville 420 champion Dale Earnhardt, Wrangler Jeans Pontiac, 103.005 mph; Harry Gant, Skoai Bandit

Pontiac, 102.976 mph; Richard STP Buick, 102.946 mph; and Alexander, Rogers Auto Leasing 102.725 mph.

Left: After that night at Nashville, Mark modified his chassis geometry based on what he had seen and his intuition. It worked. He won the pole when he returned to Nashville for his third race.

Right: Jackie and Julian watch Mark's Daytona practice session from the top of the hauler in the garage area. Jackie recorded Mark's lap times and Julian manned the radio.

Mark underestimated the physical stamina and chassis set-up required for Nashville's hot, 420-lap race. His face is flushed with heat and exertion. Richard Petty and Ricky Rudd are exiting the pits in the background.

drill some holes in the floorboard," Inman told Mark. "Because you're going to melt and run out of that thing tonight."

"Oh, did that ever insult me," Mark recalls today. "I was going to show 'em what the deal was. When the green flag came out, *Varoom!*, I went in the lead. I led the first thirty-six laps. But then the handling went away. It felt like I had four flat tires. I didn't know how to set the car up for the long haul. I was a lap down before the first caution and after another sixty laps I got lapped again. I finally finished eleventh. I was five laps down. It was the most humiliating defeat I'd ever had. I got so tired, I thought I was going to die. I had never experienced anything like that. But I learned something."

Darrell Waltrip, who won the race, was also battered by the heat. He conducted the winner's interview flat on his back, his right leg extended in the air while a crewman massaged it and his wife, Stevie, applied a bandage to his blistered heel.

But the heat wasn't Mark's biggest problem.

"The kid made a mistake setting his seat too far back," veteran crew chief Harry Hyde told Joe Caldwell of the *Nashville Banner*. "He fixed it where it was comfortable in practice and just sitting in the car. He'd never run a race this long and he didn't know that the longer the race goes, the more the forces keep pushing you sideways and backwards. It wasn't long until he was having trouble reaching the pedals.

"He ain't bigger than a half-dollar anyway, and spent most of the race having to tiptoe to reach the pedals," said Hyde, who had worked with Mark's team during the Nashville race. "The longer the race went, the lower down in the seat he got. I told him that if we had forty more laps to go, there wouldn't have been anything left of him to see. As it was, by the time it was over, there was only a couple of inches of helmet sticking up above the side window."

NASCAR made things worse after the race when inspectors singled out Mark's engine for a partial tear-down. They found nothing amiss.

Another dominant win at the ASA's Redbud 300, held before a standing-room-only crowd at the quarter-mile Anderson Speedway. Mark won from the pole, set the fastest race time and led 169 of 300 laps.

From Nashville, Mark hauled his Pontiac Winston Cup car more than 400 miles back to Indiana. He modified the styling, added more duct work and moved the weight in the car. And he raced elsewhere. He had won an ASA race at Cayuga International Speedway in June and he added another one—The Redbud 300 at Anderson Speedway in Indiana—in August.

On August 1, Mark made his debut on the high banks of Talladega Superspeedway in the ARCA 200. He stayed among the leaders early in the race and once in the lead, he began pulling away. He averaged more than 200 MPH during the final ten laps. His final lap of 201.5 MPH was faster than the pole-winning lap. He won by four seconds.

Mark's fourth Winston Cup race of 1981 was on September 13 at Richmond Fairgrounds Raceway. A few weeks earlier, Mark had let Morgan Shepherd drive his car at Michigan, and Shepherd had crashed.

"After we got it back together after this horrendous wreck, we went to Richmond. And we sat on the pole again," says Mark. But on race day, the team made another rookie mistake.

"One of the guys who worked for me put a rag down in the carburetor and then forgot about it," Mark recalls. "It wouldn't crank." He lost a lap right away and eventually finished seventh, two laps behind the winner.

Mark's final Winston Cup race that year was the Old Dominion 500 at Martinsville Speedway on September 27. He qualified fifth. He stayed with the leaders and even led thirty-nine laps. He finished third, three laps down. He had his top-five finish.

Mark Martin Claims Second Pole Of Season

BY GENE GRANGER
Associate Editor

RICHMOND, Va. (Sept. 11)—Mark Martin, who is making only his fourth NASCAR Winston Cup appearance, today won his second pole position.

It wasn't a complete surprise in that Darrell Waltrip had predicted it would be "among Mark, Bobby Allison, Harry Gant and me."

The 22-year-old Martin, driving a Pontiac owned by Bob Reeder of Denver, Colo., turned a lap of 93.435 mph around the 0.542-mile Richmond Fairgrounds Raceway to win the No. 1 starting spot for the Wrangler Sanfor-Set 400.

"Don't ask me about winning the pole yet," smiled Martin before the conclusion of time trials. "There are still a lot of guys who have yet to run. These big guys are pretty sneaky. They always find a way to come up with a little more speed."

Maybe, but not today.

"We weren't really surprised," Martin added. "We had been running some pretty good laps in practice. But I try to be a realistic person. I think my chances of winning the race are very slim. I just want to run good.

"I can learn tremendously from a race like this and so can the men who work with me. That's one of the reasons we are here."

Martin, from North Liberty, Ind., is a regular competitor for the American Speed Association (ASA) a midwest circuit. "We run 20 races on 10 different tracks and it's like a small NASCAR," Martin said.

The big question was, where did Richard Petty qualify?

"Who won the pole? Mark Martin? And I didn't even make the field. Maybe

I am getting too old for this sort of thing," Petty shrugged. (Twenty of the race's 32 starting positions were determined today.)

Neither did Kyle Petty, Richard's son and the other half of the STP Buick team. Kyle blew an engine in practice and was unable to qualify.

that has qualified well before. I thought I could beat him this time. I thought I had something, but it just wasn't enough."

Waltrip still leads the Busch Pole Awards with six. No other driver has more than two. With only seven more poles to be contested, Waltrip appears to

---

Below: Mark dominated at the end of the race to win the ARCA 200 at Talladega on August 1. His last lap of 201.5 MPH was actually faster than the pole-winning speed. His margin of victory was more than four seconds.

"I had baby brakes at Martinsville," Mark says today. "Chevrolet disc brakes were baby brakes. Everyone else had these huge, old, expensive brakes. But Chevrolet brakes were free. You went to the junkyard and got the calipers off a junked car, worked on 'em and put 'em on. The brake pads were 3/8th of an inch thick. The pads today are one-inch thick. And I ran the whole race and finished third using these little baby brakes."

His final NASCAR effort for the 1981 season came in the Sportsman race at Charlotte Motor Speedway, where he finished second.

"I won something like $15,100 to run second in that Sportsman race at Charlotte, and it was the most money I'd ever won," Mark recalls. "I thought I was on my way. I had sat on two Winston Cup poles. I'd run third at Martinsville and finished seventh at Richmond.

"We'd had that historic season in 1980 with the new Mark II car. But in 1981, we stood some people on their ears, too. And at the end of the 1981 season, Waddell Wilson called me to come drive the No. 28 car. And I turned him down. I turned down the 28 car. I should have taken the deal. The 28 car has always been good. But the 28 car didn't impress me.

"Besides, I was going to do it on my own. I'm talking about using some common sense logic. I figured if I sat on two poles in five races, I should sit on ten or fifteen for a whole season, right? And if I'd run third already, then shortly I was going to win. It didn't matter if I didn't have a sponsor. I'd get a sponsor as soon as I won. And so I told Waddell, 'No, I'm going to do my own deal.'

"That's how little I knew about what was fixin' to happen."

"We were just swallowed up."

Almost immediately after the sportsman race in Charlotte in early October 1981, Mark began laying the groundwork for his first full season in the Winston Cup series and his campaign for rookie of the year. He wanted Ray Dillon to join him.

"We sat and talked about it at length," recalls Dillon. "Hindsight is 20-20. Who knows what would have happened had I packed up and moved to Charlotte. But I had an established business in Indiana that was profitable and my customer base was there. I elected not to go."

Steve Peterson, who is now technical director of NASCAR Winston Cup, was then a Dillon employee, hired in early 1980 at Mark's request. He remembers the conversation when Mark returned to Indiana in late November in 1981 and announced that he needed to build a car.

"I can tell you that Dillon has no interest in that project," Peterson said.

"I know. Look, will you help me build a car?" Mark pleaded. Peterson said yes.

"It started out as him and I and one other guy on Thanksgiving weekend in 1981," Peterson says. "We had to do it all without interfering with Dillon's production. So we had to work during Dillon's vacation schedule. We worked almost twenty-four hours a day. But by the time the weekend was over and Dillon's people started back to work, we had built a Winston Cup frame and chassis with the interior cage and sheet metal. Mark's dad showed up at midnight Sunday with a truck and trailer. We loaded that thing in the back of the truck and that was just about the end of the Dillon-Mark Martin era."

Says Julian: "Mark got me to pitch in and help finish it before we loaded it. And every tool that I picked up was sticky with the blood from his hands. There wasn't any particular reason.

He'd just worn through the skin to the blood. When we finally got loaded and headed toward Charlotte, I guess Mark slept all the way down there."

That brand of personal involvement, so evident throughout Mark's career, was soon a thing of the past as he moved to North Carolina and began doing things as they did in NASCAR racing. His mother, Jackie, came with him to be his business manager.

In January, Mark introduced a new crew chief, Bobby Jones, and held a press conference to announce sponsorship from Apache Stove, a small manufacturer of wood- and coal-burning stoves in North Carolina. The full season sponsorship was for $50,000. The best teams then were getting $300,000 to $400,000.

"But that's all that we could come up with, so we made the deal because we needed it," Mark says. "Besides, I still felt like we were going to be in good shape because we were going to be on the Winner's Circle program shortly."

With Jones in charge, Mark stopped directing his team's strategy. He stopped working on the race cars. In fact, he had been asked *not* to come to the shop. He was now the driver, not the boss.

Peterson says, "When Bobby Jones kicked Mark out of his own shop, he didn't want him to be a distraction. But that was a huge change for Mark. He wasn't the same Mark. He wasn't totally focused and working on the race car. Once Mark got kicked out, he didn't feel like he could come back. He felt like he had to get the people to do the job."

Mark's first race that season was the Busch Clash. He had qualified for the race by winning the pole position at Nashville the previous July. Mark was the first rookie ever to qualify for the Clash.

Above: The Apache Stove sponsorship announcement on January 27, 1982 was a media event at Charlotte Motor Speedway. From left to right, Mark, Darrell Waltrip, Speedway president Humpy Wheeler, and the Apache Stove model.

Left: The graphics made Mark's hauler one of the most eye-catching rigs of the 1982 season. The Apache sponsorship deal was for $50,000—six times less than top teams' budgets. That, unfortunately, was academic because Apache never paid Mark anything, and the deal was abandoned.

"Those last five laps in the Clash were fun," he said afterwards. He finished a modest eighth, but said, "I haven't enjoyed driving a race car that much in five years." It would be years before he could say that again.

"We ran like crud during Speedweeks," Mark recalls. "My car was built wrong. It was built with the frame rails too close to the ground. NASCAR never checked until qualifying day, and then all of a sudden they ran the block under there and our car was one full inch too low."

The team fixed it, but there was tremendous tension. Mark qualified twenty-sixth and finished 30th in the Daytona 500, dropping out after 75 laps with a broken engine. At the end of Speedweeks, Mark released Jones.

"On Sunday evening at the end of the race, not only had we run like crud, but I had to let the guy go who was my leader," Mark says. "And we never got the money from Apache Stoves. We left their decals on the car until June, but that prevented us from getting anything else. I left Daytona broke, both spiritually and financially. I guess I never really recovered from that in 1982."

Above: Buddy Baker offers Mark some of his experience racing at Daytona as they talked in the garage area before the Busch Clash. **Right:** The Busch Clash on February 2 was the first race of 1982. The leader board shows Mark in ninth place. He later passed Morgan Shepherd to take eighth. Jackie identified the cars by number on the photo: 98 (Shepherd), 02 (Mark), and 9 (Bill Elliott).

Recalls Peterson: "We started out with a lot of hope and enthusiasm. But we had a lot of problems in races—pit stop problems and engine problems."

"After Daytona," Mark says, "we went to Richmond and ran bad. We finished eighteen laps down at Bristol. We went to Atlanta and had electrical problems. We went to Rockingham and because we weren't fast enough, I got frustrated and crashed the car. And then we went to Darlington and the boys left a plug wire off and I ran the 500 miles on seven cylinders and finished seventh. And it went that way for the rest of the year. We had a few respectable runs, but it was nothing like we expected."

By mid-season, when the series returned to Nashville in July, the problems had mushroomed into an endless, full-scale crisis. Only one year earlier, Mark had won his first pole position. "Now we were totally disorganized as a team," recalls Peterson. "People were doubting Mark. Jackie had bills to pay. And Julian had no money to pay them."

Bad pit stops were a constant problem during 1982. Here Mark leaves the pits after stopping for fuel and tires during the Valleydale 500 at Bristol. He finished eighteen laps down in fourteenth place.

Recalls Julian: "It was hard in business at that particular time and I had nearly a million dollars borrowed from an outfit that I was fairly certain was a Mafia-backed outfit. I was paying 28 $^1/_2$ percent on the loan—$28.50 on every $100 I was taking in. I was strapped out."

The team's problems were compounded in July when Mark's transporter was involved in a freeway crash in Georgia. No one was seriously hurt. Mark's car was not damaged. But the truck was undrivable.

"That took a bunch of money and bunch of time that needed to be going to racing, not building another hauler," Julian says.

Recalls Mark: "Darrell Waltrip pleaded with me to drop back to a partial schedule where I could catch my breath and get my feet set. I wouldn't do it. I was too stubborn. I wanted to be one of the full-schedule boys."

By today's standards, Mark had an impressive rookie year. Even by 1982 standards, it was good. He finished fourteenth in Winston Cup points and had eight top-ten finishes, including a pair of fifth places at Dover in May and Riverside in the season-ending race in November. By contrast, Ricky Craven won the 1995 rookie title with four top-ten finishes and by finishing twenty-fourth in Winston Cup points. But Mark had been the odds-on favorite to win the rookie of the year title in 1982. He lost to Geoff Bodine.

"I made up my mind I was going to win rookie of the year no matter what," Mark says. "And when I didn't... Just nothing turned out. We got lapped in every race. I ran the whole season begging and borrowing. It killed me. It broke me financially and it destroyed me. We were just swallowed up."

Right: To make some much-needed money, Mark supplied one of the team's cars for use in filming "Stroker Ace." Julian drove the car at Charlotte, where he posed with actor Burt Reynolds and producer Hal Needham at the far right.

Mark knew one thing now. He no longer wanted to be an owner. He wanted to drive for someone else, or no one at all.

Around Christmas, car owner J.D. Stacy called and asked Mark to drive his No. 2 Buick. Mark was thrilled. This was a winning car. In fact, Tim Richmond had won the final race of 1982 in Stacy's Buick. "Little did I know that Stacy was through pouring dough into the team and that (crew chief) Dale Inman was leaving," Mark says. "Stacy was pulling the plug and all the good people were trying to leave."

At Daytona, Mark qualified Stacy's car twelfth for his second Daytona 500, but crashed on lap 136 and finished 28th. "We went to Atlanta and I remember clearly what happened," Mark says.

"We qualified twelfth, and in the race I ran in tenth for awhile. And then I started coming. We got the car adjusted right and I went from tenth to third. And then came the last pit stop of the day. And for some reason, I felt like I knew they had used all of their new tires. We were racing. We were almost there. I could see the front. And I said, 'Don't you guys put used tires on this car.' And they put our practice tires back on because they were out of new tires. Somehow or another, I was afraid that was going to happen. I finished seventh."

After Atlanta, there was an off-weekend in the Winston Cup series, and at 10 AM Saturday, April 2, at Charlotte Motor Speedway, an auctioneer started his sing-song chant and began liquidating the Mark Martin Racing Team.

"I had built a huge debt throughout the 1982 season," Mark says. "And I'd taken one huge whipping. I had an auction and I auctioned everything I owned. Every tool, every part, every piece, my transmissions, my gears, trailers, maybe as many as four cars, everything. I don't remember a whole lot about it. Everybody came. I've had a lot of people tell me I looked pretty sad. I was just embarrassed and humiliated."

The salve to Mark's pride came the next weekend at Darlington Raceway. He had some of his best races on this tough South Carolina track in 1981 and 1982, and it smiled on him again.

In April 1983 Mark Martin Racing was put up for auction to repay the large debts from 1982. This was a painful day for the entire Martin family. Everything was sold, from race cars to spark plugs.

"We qualified tenth and we ran great," Mark says. "We were in the top five all day long. And we finished third, but I felt like I had a chance to race for the win at the end and we blew it." A decision to pit for tires during a late-race caution cost Mark the chance to get close enough to the leaders to race them.

It was, nonetheless, his best career finish. But he was not in good spirits. He was mad about the pit stop strategy. And he was mad at Ricky Rudd, who despite being a lap down had held up Mark in the final laps.

When the series went to North Wilkesboro, Mark and Rudd tangled

RACE CAR AUCTION SALE
SATURDAY, APRIL 2, 1983 — 10:00 A.M.
MARK MARTIN RACING, OWNER
CHARLOTTE, NORTH CAROLINA

SALE LOCATION: Charlotte Motor Speedway Building, Harrisburg, N.C.–Hwy 29 and Morehead Rd.

RACE CARS	RACE CAR PARTS	BLADES, ALTERNATORS, START- ERS, HEADERS, TAIL PIPES, ETC.	12 TON SHOP PRESS RAZORBACK PORTABLE WASHER
1982 BUICK REGAL (BUILT BY MIKE	11 GRAND NATIONAL REAR ENDS		CENTRAL H.D. METAL BANDSAW

and Mark put Rudd into the wall on the fifty-ninth lap. "Then my car broke anyway, even after I put Ricky into the wall," Mark says. "Then we go to Martinsville and the controversy is sort of swirling about Ricky and I, and I'm feeling a lot of pressure. And at Martinsville, I tangled with

Earnhardt. He chopped me off, and he spun and I spun. I got hit. So I ran along crippled for awhile until the engine blew up."

After the Martinsville race, Mark Martin was fired. In seven races, he had started no worse than twelfth. He had two top-ten finishes, including a third place at Darlington. But Harrington wanted a winner right away. "I felt like we were running out of time and needed a more experienced driver," he said at the time. "Mark is a young kid and has plenty of determination. He'll make it. I don't feel like I have the time for Mark to develop. I want to win tomorrow." He hired Morgan Shepherd.

Mark was devastated. "I thought everything was all right after Atlanta and Darlington," he said at the time. "I've got to look for a ride to keep active. I have no car of my own to go back to. The thing with Stacy has really hurt me. I have no conception of what I'm going to do now."

A week after being fired, Mark drove for car owner D.K. Ulrich at Talladega. Ulrich's Chevy was not as good as Stacy's Buick. Mark qualified twenty-fifth and blew his engine on the sixty-fifth lap. He crashed at Nashville a week later, and that was it with Ulrich.

Mark missed the next two races, but got a ride for the World 600 at Charlotte in a Chevrolet owned by Emanuel Zervakis. He started twentieth and crashed on lap 279. He missed two more races, then got a ride with a new team, Morgan-McClure Racing. Co-owners Tim Morgan and Larry McClure were fielding an Oldsmobile in a limited schedule and Mark was behind the wheel at Michigan on June 19. He blew an engine and finished twenty-seventh. He drove the car five more times that year, and his best performance came at Talladega, where he finished tenth, two laps down.

"I was in the No. 4 car, but the only problem was this was before they had anything," Mark says. "At the end of the season, I never called them back. And they never called me back. I didn't want to drive for them, and they didn't want me to drive for them."

Shepherd never won in the Stacy car. At the end of the year, the team folded. For Mark, the bottom had fallen out. It was one shade of failure to lose your team, but quite another to lose your

career. With no prospects and plenty of free time, he began drinking to excess. He would drink himself into oblivion and not remember it the next day.

"When I first started drinking beer, it was with Trickle at the races," Mark says. "Everybody always picked on me and teased me because I drank so little. I'd drink three-quarters of an inch off the top of a beer and by then it would be hot. My dad drank. He worked his guts out every single day, but he drank. And at times, he drank every night. Even before I started racing, my dad drank heavy at times. It affected my life. I was always scared of my dad's volatile demeanor when he was drunk. I was always scared that he'd go off."

"That's what tore my parents' marriage apart. It was the only thing I disliked about my father, what alcohol did to him. My father hasn't had a drink in ten years, but he is an alcoholic. I always said that I wasn't ever going to be like him in that respect. But I had a serious bout with alcoholism as well."

"It's important that people know how this happened. I didn't like alcohol, especially because of my

father's drinking. But I went from drinking so little I couldn't even keep from being teased about it, to where I almost even enjoyed it a little bit, to having some fun once and awhile, like a normal drinker does, to drinking in excess. Alcoholism is like a disease that grows to maturity. You get to a certain point where you can't control it."

"The NASCAR thing is what sunk me. That's when alcohol got me, because I was so distraught over the whole thing. Everything was just going down the tubes. I was so heartbroken and down. I was really, really angry and bitter about what had happened, and I drank a lot. A lot of times every night. And usually I didn't stop until I went to bed. Once I started, I couldn't quit."

"I drank too much from 1982 until late 1988. When I got hooked up with Jack Roush and finally got a shot at having it all, after losing everything you could ever dream of, I guess that was the hope I needed to straighten things out and make a better life for myself and my family. I wanted to quit for awhile before I did quit. I wanted to be a controlled drinker so that I could be with people who drank, so that I could be normal in that respect. But that's not an option for a person who can't stop once they've started."

Mark quit on his own. "I had to find something else, and that's how my focus went into physical fitness," Mark says. "I let one thing go and focused on something else. I'm not ashamed of it. I'm just glad it's over with. Now I'm up at 5:45 in the morning and in the gym at six, then out by 7 or 7:10. This is five days a week, Monday through Friday. Even after a 500 mile race the day before, I'm throwing iron at six Monday morning."

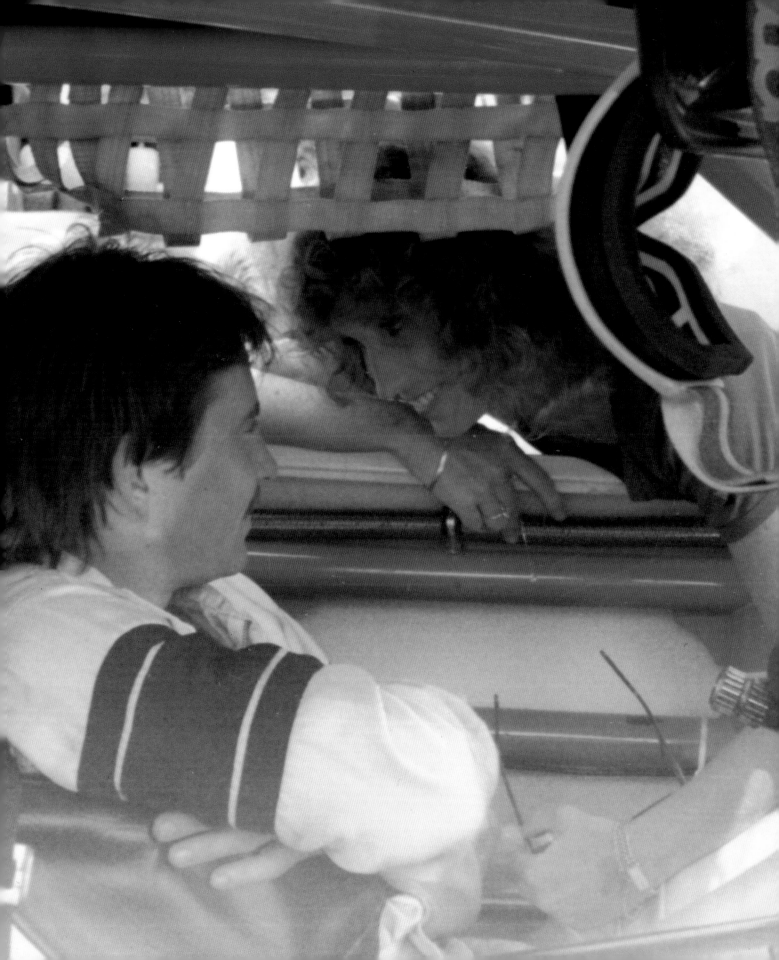

CHAPTER ELEVEN

"My life is fulfilled."

Above: Mark's sister, Glenda, had long thought her friend Arlene (left) would be a good match for Mark. **Left:** Glenda was right. Mark and Arlene first met for dinner in late 1983, and afterward spent many hours talking on the telephone. By January 1984 they were dating. Arlene was not a race fan when she met Mark, but on her first trip to Daytona in February she was dazzled by what she saw.

As 1983 came to a close, Mark's racing career was in shambles, but his personal life was about to take a dramatic turn. Back in Batesville for Christmas, Mark had a blind date with a friend of Glenda's named Arlene.

"I didn't want to meet him," Arlene recalls. "I really liked Glenda and I was afraid I might not like her brother. And Mark was younger than I was—five and a half years younger. He had never been married and didn't have children. I had four kids. I was divorced. And at that point in my life, I was just kind of sick of men."

Oh, and one other little problem.

"I really didn't know anything about auto racing," she says. "I thought it was pretty ignorant to drive around in a circle."

Arlene finally decided to go ahead and meet Mark. After all, it was just dinner. And he was just visiting. "He was real nice," she recalls. "He was real humble. He was really shy, and sort of quiet. He wasn't anything like I pictured him to be. He talked some. But mostly he sat there and listened. We really didn't talk about racing much at all. When he took me home, he walked me up to the door and said goodnight. He didn't try to kiss me. I remember thinking, 'What's wrong with him?' He was like, *too* nice."

Recalls Mark, "Given the state of mind I was in at the time, I don't know how I would have ever been interested in a woman with four children. But from the minute I met her, I was attracted to her. I was single and twenty-four years old. She was in her late twenties, with four children. Other than that, she was the perfect girl for me. She was slim, she was beautiful, and she had a heart of gold. She was a fine person. I was playing the field at the time, and getting rather tired of that. I found out that the girls I thought were dream girls really weren't. And I was feeling awfully lonely and alone. I was open to the idea of settling down with one, solid, honest person.

"For the week I was in Arkansas, I chased Arlene around. And she wouldn't go out with me. She let me come over to her house and we'd sit and talk. So she would spend time with me, but she wouldn't date me."

As for his racing career, "I was in trouble," Mark says. "I didn't have a sponsor. I didn't have any money. And a bunch of people who had given me stuff before wouldn't give it to me anymore. And then my dad stepped in and he bought me two race cars, which were $15,000 each at the time. And Ron Neal, who supplied my engines in the ASA days, started talking with me.

"He said, 'You know what we need to do? We need to build a Ford.' Nobody had run a Ford in short-track racing forever. They just weren't competitive. But Ford was getting back into racing, so we went and sat down with Lee Morse, who was a big player in their motorsports program. Lee was a big short-track fan, and he knew of me, so he kicked us some motor parts and different things out the back door. And Ron Neal built my engines for a whole year and didn't charge me anything. I owe a lot of thanks to those three — Ron Neal, Lee Morse, and my dad—because if it wasn't for them, I don't know what I would have done."

At the Minnesota State Fair on Labor Day Mark posed with Arlene and her four daughters. From left to right, Arlene, turning to the camera, Rachel (11), Stacy (8), on Mark's lap, and Heather (11) peeking over the shoulder of Amy (13).

Mark turned his sights backwards, and made a deal to drive in the ASA series in 1984 for car owner Randy Rieble of Beaver Dam, Wisconsin.

"The deal was I would come drive for him and he'd pay me just enough to live on," Mark says. "I'd bring race cars and I'd bring free engines, and he would supply one race car and everything else."

Mark moved to Wisconsin. But he could not get Arlene out of his mind. He frequently called her on the telephone.

Arlene says, "Mark and I became friends first. That was one of the secrets to the relationship. I got to know him. He would call me several times a week and we would talk for an hour or two on the phone. We'd talk about all kinds of different things. It didn't center around what he did."

Mark returned to Batesville in January. It was his sister's birthday, but he was also eager to see Arlene again.

"This time, I kinda broke through," Mark says. When he asked her to go to Daytona with him for Speedweeks, she agreed. They drove there in a van, Mark in search of a ride for the Daytona 500.

He didn't find a ride. He was now just a spectator — one among thousands in the infield. He

In Randy Rieble's shop in Beaver Dam, Wisconsin, Mark tightens the fittings on a length of braided steel hose. Rieble made a deal with Mark to run his Thunderbird, and Mark provided two cars of his own and engines from Prototype.

had raced at Daytona. Now he stood with the fans on the main road through the infield, watching the activity in the garage. He couldn't get in. He didn't have a pass. He didn't really want one — not without a car to go with it. It was a moment he will never forget. But it was just a moment. "I was positive about what little bit I had," he says. "I was going to get back out there."

And he and Arlene had a good time at Daytona. "I had never been to a race," she recalls. "I could not believe all the people there. I could not believe that many people liked auto racing. It amazed me it was that popular."

By then, Mark knew he wanted to marry Arlene. He told her so on the ride home. She visited him in Wisconsin and knew she was in love. He proposed in the spring. She accepted, and they married on October 27, 1984.

"She married me for me, that's for sure," Mark says. "Because there wasn't much else in my future right then. There was no hope of the kind of life we have now. In 1984, I only won one race and one pole in the ASA series. I had lost touch. It took me a while to get back on my feet and get the setups figured out. They'd downsized the cars and they were different."

In late 1984, Mark received a call from Benny Ertel, who today is Mark's business manager.

"At that time I was the team coordinator for Bobby Allison's short-track program," Ertel said. "Jerry Gunderman was the owner. Well, the team got the bug to go full-time racing in ASA, and they wanted a full-time driver. Crew chief Jim Fennig said, 'Why don't we call Mark Martin?' We

Left: Mark sat on the outside pole at the Milwaukee Mile in 1984. Dick Trickle won the pole, and Alan Kulwicki, behind Mark in the Hardee's car, started fourth. Below: At the Winston Cup race at Atlanta in November Mark impressed many fans when he put his car on the outside pole, next to Bill Elliott. Engine problems led to a twenty-eighth-place finish.

For 1987, Mark ran a full season in NASCAR's Busch series with Bruce Lawmaster's team. This reunited Mark with his ex-brother-in-law, David Lovendahl, who was crew chief. The win at Dover was Ford's first Busch victory.

had seen Mark in his ASA championship days and we knew him when he was in Winston Cup. The team's reaction was, 'Oh yeah, Mark Martin is going to drive for us. Sure.' Because Mark was already driving for Rieble we weren't sure he'd be available."

Mark jumped at the opportunity. Ertel called Ray Dillon, who agreed to provide cars. But to join Gunderman, Mark had to break his two-year contract with Rieble.

"I was the one who asked for the contract," Mark says. "But I had to go. I had to get back on the top of my game—my life. So I just went. I went and made a deal with Gunderman and moved, and then I went back and offered a settlement to Rieble, which amounted to probably about $30,000 worth of stuff. My tax return that year showed that I made $19,000. I was still in the hole. I'd used up all my favors—everything I could possibly use. I did the wrong thing with that contract. I did what I had to do. I was desperate—like somebody who doesn't steal, but rather than starve to death, he might take some food."

"Jerry Gunderman offered me a brighter future. And Gunderman gave me two great years. Jimmy Fennig was my crew chief. He was a great racer. In 1985, we finished fourth for the ASA title, but we won four races and six poles. And in 1986, we won seven poles and five races, and the championship."

It was Mark's fourth ASA title. And as with the Mark II chassis, he had pioneered a new way of winning in ASA, this time with a Ford.

Before the 1987 season opened, Mark decided to make another stab at NASCAR racing. He had

Right: When Jack Roush decided to race in NASCAR he chose Mark as his driver. "Mark was the only one who was more interested in who was going to work on the car and what kind of cars they were going to be and how much money we were going to spend on testing, rather than how much money he was going to make."

run five races for Gunderman in the Winston Cup series in 1986, with little success. For 1987, he agreed to drive a Ford owned by Bruce Lawmaster in the full twenty-seven-race Busch Grand National series, which is one step below Winston Cup. Mark and his family moved to Greensboro, North Carolina.

Mark says, "This offered a great opportunity if it worked. But if it didn't. . . I wasn't anxious to leave again and come back to nothing. I didn't know if I could do that again."

Mark's ex-brother-in-law, David Lovendahl, was the crew chief. Mark says, "We raced a heavy V-8 Ford against light V-6 Chevrolets and Buicks, so it was not very likely that we would have a barn-burning season. But we shined pretty bright." When he won at Dover in May 1987, it was the first for Ford in the series. He also won at Orange County Speedway in North Carolina and at Richmond. After four years back in stock car's minor leagues, he was on the verge of returning to the Winston Cup series.

In mid-1987, he began talking to veteran Winston Cup mechanic Steve Hmiel about forming a team. Hmiel was from upstate New York and had learned the sport working at Petty Enterprises.

Hmiel says, "In some small ways Mark Martin was actually more appealing to an everyday person like me after what happened to him in 1982 than he was in 1981. In 1982, you could tell this kid was struggling. He was working his guts out. I felt more comfortable around some guy who had stubbed his toe like the rest of us had."

"I was leaving Michigan after the June race, when I was approached by someone from Ford and asked if I would be interested in running a Ford team for a guy really well connected at Ford. I said yeah. Two weeks later, Jack Roush called."

Jack Roush, a former Ford engineer, had become a multi-millionaire with his own automotive businesses. Roush was also a racer. His sports cars had won IMSA and SCCA championships. Now Roush wanted to race in the big leagues — NASCAR's Winston Cup series. He asked Hmiel to find a building and begin organizing a team. Hmiel thought Roush was kidding, and he didn't do anything. Only when Roush called a week later for an update did Hmiel realize he was serious. Together with Robin Pemberton, another Petty Enterprises graduate, Hmiel got to work.

"It was real hard to get the program going," Hmiel recalls. "We had to build shop space. We had to build race cars. We had to organize an engine program. We had to get trucks and trailers."

"As for a driver, I was just sure that everybody shared the same thoughts on Mark that I did. But it was a tough sell. I pushed for Mark and I pushed for Mark and I pushed for Mark. But understandably, Jack couldn't sell a sponsor as easily on two new crew chiefs *and* a new driver. But Jack was like me. He liked what he saw in Mark."

"For months, I never talked to Jack," says Mark. "I talked to Steve. And probably around September, I finally called Steve and said, 'I gotta know something. I have to make a decision.'"

Mark finally scheduled a meeting with Roush in early October at Roush's headquarters in Livonia, Michigan.

"I went up there and we talked and looked and talked and talked and talked and stood up and shook hands and had a deal," Mark recalls.

Roush, a small man, says: "I guess I had more empathy and compassion for what he was trying to do because he was more nearly my own size than bigger drivers. Small people seem like they have to scratch for more things."

Roush considered a number of drivers, but "Mark was the only one who was more interested in who was going to work on the car and what kind of cars they were going to be and how much money we were going to spend on testing, rather than how much money he was going to make."

Mark says, "I was excited about the prospect of driving for Jack Roush. And he had the crew chief I wanted. I wanted Steve because I thought he wanted me. It was more important for him to want me than for him to be good. I had already been somewhere where I wasn't wanted. I didn't want to be anywhere where I wasn't wanted ever again."

Their first year together was a struggle. Mark finished fifteenth in points—one position lower than his disastrous 1982 campaign.

"The first year was tough," Mark says. "It's pretty hard with new teams and we didn't have anybody with a notebook to tell us what we should be doing." Mark finished second at Bristol in April, and in September he won the pole at Dover. That same month, he finished fourth at Richmond.

"He was carrying the cars and carrying the team on his back," says Roush. "Mark was an incredible driver. He was like an experienced, journeyman Winston Cup driver, and that I hadn't expected."

Mark says, "We ran good, but we didn't run as good as we expected to run. In 1989, that changed for the better. We changed our chassis setup strategy dramatically and tested about eighteen times. There was no limit then. Once we got a season worth of mistakes behind us, and had a winter to catch our breath and rebuild, it all came around."

Actually, the 1989 season started slowly for the team. But Mark won the pole at Darlington in April and finished fourth in the race. And then he won the pole at Bristol the next week and finished sixth. He finished third at North Wilkesboro and was sixth at Martinsville. At Talladega, he won the pole and finished third; in Charlotte, he finished sixth. He won another pole at Dover and finished second.

Mark won his fifth pole at Daytona in July and led twenty-eight laps before running out of fuel late in the race. He was third at Pocono and third at Talladega, where he won his sixth pole of the season. He finished second at Watkins Glen after a spirited duel with Rusty Wallace. He finished second in the Southern 500, and second at Dover, after leading laps 415 to 444 and battling Dale Earnhardt to the check-

At the final race in Atlanta an oil line ruptured on lap 202 and Mark's car burst into flames. Mark finished third in final 1989 Winston Cup point standings behind champion Rusty Wallace and runner-up Dale Earnhardt.

An exuberant Jack Roush (left) and Steve Hmiel celebrate at Rockingham. Mark's career first Winston Cup win was also the first win for the Roush team.

ered flag. He was in the winning zone now. And at Charlotte, it looked as if it would finally happen.

"We had Charlotte won," Mark says. "And then a darn tire went down with fifteen to go. We had a ten-second lead. It was a hard pill to swallow." Ken Schrader took the victory. Mark was third.

At Rockingham, on October 22, 1989, he finally broke through. Mark led the final seventy-seven laps of the AC-Delco 500 and won by 2.98 seconds over Rusty Wallace. He had started seventh, but didn't really come on until the final 100 laps, when he took charge of the race.

"I can't believe it," he said in victory lane. "My life is fulfilled. I feel like I'm the luckiest man alive."

Today, Mark recalls, "We ran competitive, but we really finished off strong. We didn't lead the most laps, but we beat Rusty Wallace at Rockingham. That's pretty hard to do. I did say that my life was fulfilled because I felt it in my heart. That was what my life had been about since 1974 and it was the hardest thing any human being could have ever done, going what I had gone through, being knocked to the ground and starting from scratch and clawing my way back to a Winston Cup win. It was 1989 and I'd been racing a long, long, long time and wanted to win. And I thought it was possible for a long time. It was a big accomplishment."

"We ran second five times that year," says Hmiel. "We felt like, 'Darn, are we ever going to win a race?' But we won at Rockingham and wound up third in points in our second year of racing. That was unbelievable."

CHAPTER TWELVE

Above: Mark captured his second Winston Cup win at Richmond, but the smiles didn't last long. NASCAR officials determined that the carburetor spacer bolted to the manifold was a half-inch too thick. The team was fined $40,000 and Mark was penalized forty-six Winston Cup points. *Left:* Arlene gives Mark some encouragement before the race at Charlotte in October. Mark qualified sixth and finished fourteenth, running on seven cylinders.

"I lived points real hard."

From the depths of racing oblivion, Mark Martin would, in 1990, come very close to reaching the top in stock-car racing. He lost the Winston Cup championship to Dale Earnhardt by twenty-six points. That is the difference between first and seventh place in a single race.

When fans discuss that year's battle, the discussion invariably turns to the forty-six points that were stripped from Mark and his team after their victory at Richmond in March. Those points made the difference between winning and losing the title.

But the forty-six points were stripped from Mark in the second race of the year. He had almost the entire season to make them up. It just so happened that when it was all over, the margin was small enough that forty-six points would have made a difference. Earnhardt didn't back into the title. He won nine races; Mark won three.

After finishing twenty-first at Daytona, Mark qualified sixth for the race at Richmond. He took the lead for the first time with just sixteen laps to go when he scurried out of the pits ahead of everyone else after taking only two new tires. The tire strategy worked. He won the race by three seconds over Earnhardt.

But after a lengthy post-race inspection, NASCAR announced that they had found a carburetor spacer mounted on the engine's intake manifold that was one-half inch thicker than the two inches allowed. Winston Cup Director Dick Beaty fined Mark's team $40,000 and stripped him of forty-six points, though he let the victory stand. The forty-six points represented the difference between first and tenth place, which was the finishing position of the last car on the lead lap.

"All we would have had to do to be legal was to spot weld the spacer," Hmiel says. "But beyond that, it floored us. We had been through two or three inspections and suddenly what we had run all weekend was ruled illegal. That hurt. But we kept going. We didn't worry about those points. We didn't know how many we were going to win or lose by anyway."

Says Roush: "We made it to victory lane, but the price of admission was high. It's old news, but the fact is, the inspector had looked at that part three times and sealed it twice during that weekend. And there was no dimensional difference between what we ran that week and what we ran the next week. It was just how it was attached. It gave us no advantage. Everybody knew there was that conflict with the rules and knew we weren't the first people who had done what we did."

As the season progressed, Mark started racking up consistently good finishes. He was second at Darlington in April, and second at Bristol. He won the pole at North Wilkesboro and finished sixth, and was seventh at Martinsville. He was third at Talladega and third at Charlotte, fourth at Dover and second at Sears Point. Mark moved into first place in Winston Cup points, ahead of Morgan Shepherd.

He won poles at Michigan and Pocono, and through the summer kept posting enough good finishes to stay atop the points. At Michigan in August, he won his second race of the year, leading the final thirty-eight laps to win by 1.7 seconds over Greg Sacks.

"We didn't really gain that much in the points, but with this win, everybody is going to stand up and say this team is serious," he said in victory lane. After Michigan, his lead over Earnhardt in the championship was forty-eight points. And he was battling head to head with him almost every week.

When Earnhardt won the Southern 500 at Darlington Raceway, Mark was sixth. Earnhardt won again at Richmond, but Mark finished second. Mark was second at Dover; Earnhardt third. At Martinsville, Earnhardt was second while Mark, who had won the pole, was third. With five races to go, Mark still led the championship, but was only sixteen points ahead. It was a toss-up.

At North Wilkesboro, Mark took the lead from Earnhardt with thirty-seven laps to go and won by 3.63 seconds. It was his third victory of the year. Earnhardt had led the most laps and gained enough bonus points to tie Mark in total points, so there was no change in the championship battle. But it was huge confidence booster.

"We came back and beat Earnhardt when nobody expected us to," Mark says.

Both Mark and Earnhardt stumbled at Charlotte. Mark finished fourteenth. Earnhardt was twenty-fifth. Mark's lead was forty-nine points. Three races to go.

At Rockingham, they both stumbled again. Earnhardt finished tenth, Mark was eleventh. "It was like sending two big home-run hitters up against each other for a home-run hitting contest and watching both bunt," says Hmiel.

Earnhardt turned the tide at Phoenix. He dominated on the one-mile oval in the desert and won the race. Mark finished tenth. He lost fifty-one points to Earnhardt and went to the season finale six points behind.

"We lost it all right there in Phoenix," Mark says. "Those points there would have made the difference just as much as the ones in Richmond. But the reason we didn't win the championship is we just got beat. We had run third at Phoenix the year before. We knew how to run good at Phoenix. That time, we didn't run good for some reason. And we really don't know why."

Before the Atlanta race, Mark and other Ford drivers tested there.

"The fastest we could run was a 30.4 [-second lap]," Mark says. "Davey Allison had his car there, so they asked me if I wanted to drive it." Allison was out of the points race and the attitude among the Ford teams was to do anything they could to help Mark beat Earnhardt, a Chevy driver.

"The first lap I made in Davey's car was a 30.05," Mark says. "And later I ran a 30 flat. What would you have done? We asked to borrow that car with that motor."

Says Hmiel: "It was instantly faster than our car. What we did was exactly the right thing to do."

Roush agrees: "I think I'd make the same decision again."

"I lived points real hard that year," Mark says. "Other than going bankrupt, losing that champi-

Mark runs three wide in the 1991 Daytona 500 between Ken Schrader (25) and Bill Elliott (9). Mark finished twenty-first.

onship was the most humiliating kick in the teeth I've ever had. And I just won't let any points thing hurt me like that one did, because it's not necessary. There's nothing I can do about people wrecking me or tires going flat or parts breaking that shouldn't break. And I'm not going to agonize over it as bad as I did in 1990. If you focus on winning races and winning races and winning races, you can look up when it's all over with and see what the tally is. Instead of focusing on the tally, I focus on what gets you the points."

Mark told people he had finished third in 1989 and second in 1990, so the logical place to finish in 1991 was first. But the team got off to slow start and nerves became frayed. After a botched pit stop during a disappointing performance at Atlanta in March, Roush became furious with the Pemberton brothers, Robin, Ryan, and Roman. He dismissed all three, but quickly rehired Robin.

Fourth-place finishes at Darlington and Bristol helped improve the mood of the team. Mark had moved from eleventh to fourth in points. And then he won the pole at Martinsville. "We needed a

pole," Roush said that day. "We're terrible losers—every one of us. We flog ourselves in every way you can imagine when things go wrong. It may be that some of that is self-destructive. I'm not sure. But we need to continue to put enough pressure on ourselves to bring out our very best. Some of that hasn't been too pleasant."

"When things don't go good, it really tests everybody and a lot of times it tears teams apart," Mark told reporters. We've got plans to stay together for a long time."

But in a flash, the good luck turned bad again. At Martinsville, Mark never led a lap. Then his engine overheated and he dropped out after 293 of 500 laps, finishing twenty-ninth.

Then it was on to Talladega, where two and a half days of stormy weather gave way to a stormy race on the track. Even before the twenty-car crash on lap seventy-two, drivers had sensed its inevitability. Mark was right in the middle of it.

"Oh boy, I don't like this," Davey Allison had told his team on the radio as cars bobbed and weaved while racing two- and three-wide around the 2.66-mile high-banked track. Speeding off turn two on the seventy-second lap, Ernie Irvan sandwiched his car between Kyle Petty's and Mark's. Irvan tapped Petty, who spun into the pack.

After practice at Darlington, Mark checked his tires for unusual wear patterns or any irregularities that could provide hints about chassis performance. He finished fourth in the race, his first top-five of 1991.

Suddenly, Mark's Ford was simultaneously spinning and lifting off. The back end rose until the car was nearly vertical to the ground, and only the nose was touching the pavement. But instead of flipping, it came down and bounced hard on the wheels before spinning down the track. It was over in less than thirty seconds. Twenty cars, most of them badly damaged, sat steaming in soggy grass along the backstretch or on the skid-streaked pavement.

Mark gasped into his radio, "I'm OK."

Petty wasn't. He suffered a compound fracture of his left leg.

"I felt it go up," he said afterwards. "I kinda closed my eyes then. I don't like getting upside down and I was fixin' to. I thought it got upside down, but then it just landed on its feet. It gave me a pretty good jar when it landed."

Mark limped through the rest of the race and finished thirty-seven laps down in twenty-fourth place. At Charlotte, Mark won the Coca-Cola 600 pole, but a blown engine led to another DNF. But after Mark finished fifth at Dover, the team found some consistency, with a pair of thirds in June at Pocono and Michigan and a second at Pocono in July.

Back at Talladega in late July, Mark delivered one of his greatest driving displays. The Ford

teams were supposed to help one another in an effort to defeat Dale Earnhardt and the dominant Chevy teams. But long before Earnhardt sailed to victory after a final Ford attack had disintegrated, Mark had become disgusted.

He had been accommodating all afternoon, ready to draft with his fellow Ford drivers time and time again. And what had happened? No one would go with him. They had hung him out to dry.

With forty laps to go, Mark cursed on his radio and vowed to go it alone. "I promise you I'll pass every one of these [gentlemen] at least once or twice," he snarled. Mark nearly did it. Then one of his tires deflated with about twenty laps to go, relegating him to seventeenth. He still would not be deterred.

When the yellow flag flew with eight laps to go, Mark was ninth. Before the restart, there was a dispute over the line-up. Morgan Shepherd tried to take the ninth spot. Mark would have none of it.

"I ran into the side of him. I ran into the back of him. I shook my finger at him," Mark said afterwards. "I was giving him hell." An embarrassed Shepherd later told Mark: "I was just doing what they was telling me to."

At Talladega in July, Mark was in a fury. No Ford drivers would team with him in the draft to run down leader Dale Earnhardt. Working alone from seventeenth place after a flat tire, he fought his way to third. Mark is in the middle of the first row.

In the final laps, Mark battled up to third. By himself. "There at the end, the Fords wanted to work with me," he said afterwards. "I burned them all then — burned them! Forget them. I ain't no way going to work with them."

The rest of the season went up and down. Dale Earnhardt was contending for the championship again, but his challenger was Ricky Rudd. Mark was not only out of the championship hunt, he couldn't find his way into victory lane.

So when he won the pole at Charlotte in October, and began to dominate the race, it made him nervous. After leading all but thirteen of the first 211 laps, Mark's worst fears came true. Going into turn one, his engine exploded, sending pieces of metal through the oil pan. He finished thirty-fifth.

"I kinda figured something would happen to mess it up," Mark said afterwards. "It was too good to be true."

At the season finale in Atlanta, Mark broke through. He wrenched success out of a disappointing season with a 10.5-second victory over Ernie Irvan. Earnhardt clinched his fifth championship.

In the final laps, Mark's nerves got a bit frayed.

"I'm praying," he told Hmiel on the radio with ten laps to go.

"I've *been* praying," Steve replied.

This time, there were no problems.

"It got boring?" Mark asked reporters afterwards. "I meant for it to. I thought, 'I'm going to get as far ahead as I can in case something happens.'"

It was Mark's fifth career victory.

It did not alter his sixth-place finish in the Winston Cup championship. But that didn't matter.

"It's a storybook finish for us here this year," he said. "I didn't expect to win this race. That's asking too much. Stuff doesn't work out that way very often. We get to savor this one until February."

But as the team began thinking about the 1992 season, they knew it would be without one of its founders, Robin Pemberton. For Pemberton, the victory at Atlanta was bittersweet. After four years, he was saying good-bye. He left to become Kyle Petty's crew chief.

"It's going to be awful hard for the next couple of hours," Pemberton said after the race.

Above: Mark's first win of 1991 came at the last race at Atlanta. He led six times before taking the lead for good on lap 281 of 328. An unscheduled pit stop for a deflating tire early in the race put Mark a lap down, but he made it up on the next caution flag.

Right: Atlanta was the last race for crew chief Robin Pemberton (left) who moved to the Felix Sabates team and driver Kyle Petty. Team manager Steve Hmiel (right) assumed Pemberton's duties.

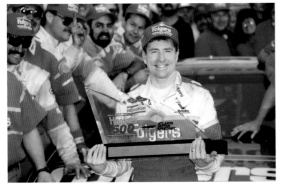

One high point of 1991 for Mark had nothing to do with racing. His son, Matthew Clyde, was born on December 17, 1991.

"Once you start winning, it's real addictive."

Robin Pemberton's departure was not the only change for 1992 season. Mark's sponsor, Folger's coffee, withdrew from the sport and was replaced by Valvoline. The switch did not change Mark's usual early-season bad luck.

In the Daytona 500, he was involved in a fourteen-car crash on the 91st lap and limped home in 29th place. A breakthrough did not come until Martinsville in April in a race remembered for cambered rear ends.

The idea was to put some camber, or angle, into the rear end to improve the angle of the tires' contact patch, particularly the right rear tire, thus providing them with bigger 'footprints' on the track—and better traction. This was accomplished by heating and bending the ordinarily straight axle tube to the desired angle.

The trick at Martinsville was putting in enough camber to work, but not so much that the increased angle stripped the splines in the hubs. Alan Kulwicki, Ernie Irvan, and Dale Earnhardt all led the race, but retired with broken rear ends. Mark took the lead from a faltering Brett Bodine on lap 474 and won by 12.12 seconds over Sterling Marlin.

"We weren't running an axle bent to the degree that some of the others had," Mark said after the race. "I'd say

During the Atlanta race weekend, the Roush team announced that Valvoline would be the new primary sponsor for 1992. Mark answered questions from the press at the track's infield media center.

our axle was bent about half as much as some of the others. We anticipated there would be some trouble with these trick rear ends."

Mark didn't win the rest of the spring and summer, but he generally finished in the top ten and almost always qualified well. And with eight races left in the 1992 season, Mark was fifth in points for the Winston Cup championship. But he was a distant 337 points behind the leader, Bill Elliott.

Four races later, after finishing second at Richmond and North Wilkesboro, Mark was still fifth in points. But now he was now only 193 points behind Elliott, who was faltering.

And in the Mello Yello 500 at Charlotte, Mark dominated the final half of the race and beat Kulwicki by 1.93 seconds for his second victory of the year. Elliott, victim of a broken sway bar, finished thirtieth. Suddenly, it was a six-way free-for-all for the championship. Mark was in fourth, only 88 points behind Elliott. Ahead of him were Kulwicki, the eventual champion, and Davey Allison. Behind him were Harry Gant, 95 points back, and Kyle Petty, 111 points behind.

"Now the championship looks like it's within reach," Mark told reporters after the race. "But we just won a big race at Charlotte Motor Speedway and points are the last thing on my mind. Right

The Roush crew pushes the new Valvoline car behind the wall for repairs at Daytona in February. A fourteen-car crash decimated the field on lap ninety-two. Mark was able to rejoin the race but finished thirty-eight laps down.

Right: At Richmond in September, Mark runs with Ken Schrader (25), Roush teammate Wally Dallenbach (16), Brett Bodine (26) and Davey Allison. Rusty Wallace drove a strong race and won by almost four seconds. Mark was second.

At Charlotte in October, Mark's second win of 1992 looked almost easy. He led six times and passed Alan Kulwicki to take the lead on lap 303 of 334. He's joined in victory lane by Rachel, Matt, Heather, and Arlene.

now we're just happy to have won a race. We've been running good enough now for a long time and finally it was our day. We just had a terrible spring and a reasonable summer and momentum has grown all year long. We raced to win last week and we'll race to win at Rockingham. We won't race for points. We'll win the championship if it's meant to be."

At Rockingham, Mark qualified second and spent the first three hours of the race doggedly running in second and third, following Petty, the eventual winner. But with only fifty-seven laps to go, he slammed into the fourth turn wall while trying to pass the lapped car driven by Michael Waltrip. His chance for the championship was gone. He finished thirtieth and fell to sixth in points, 172 behind Elliott.

"I just lost it there," he said. "I was running really hard and I just lost it."

The 1992 season had ended on a sour note. But for Mark's larger family, the NASCAR family, dark days loomed ahead in 1993.

Alan Kulwicki, who came out on top in the six-way battle for the 1992 Winston Cup championship, was killed on April Fool's Day 1993 when the twin-engine plane on which he was riding fell out of the sky while approaching the airport outside Bristol, Tennessee. And Davey Allison, the 1992 Daytona 500 winner, died on July 13 from severe head injuries he suffered when he lost control of his helicopter and crashed while attempting to land at Talladega Superspeedway.

The series went to Talladega on July 25, less than two weeks after Allison's death. The race was hardly a comfort. A huge crash in the first turn on lap seventy sent Jimmy Horton's car flying out of the track. Horton was only dazed, but another driver, Stanley Smith, was critically injured. Neil Bonnett, who had pulled the fatally injured Allison from his helicopter, chose the Talladega event as his first race back after a three-year recovery from a severe head injury he suffered at Darlington in 1990. Bonnett crashed horribly. His car flipped and careened into the front stretch fence. He was unhurt, but the race had to be stopped to fix the fence. Mark finished third. Dale Earnhardt won.

At Watkins Glen, Mark won the pole and should have had an easy win. But he began having a problem during pit stops. The hexagonal lug nuts were rounding off when tightened with high-pressure air wrenches, making them extremely difficult to get off.

"Every pit stop, we jammed at least one lug nut," Roush said afterwards. It was a mystery. Team-mate Wally Dallenbach had no problems at all with his lug nuts.

"The first stop, we lost one spot," Mark said afterwards. "The second stop, we lost about three or four spots. And the third and fourth stops, we lost the whole field. Sitting there, I was saying to myself, 'Well, there it goes.' But as soon as we got back out there, we went to work to recover."

Hmiel, who changed the right front tires, said afterwards: "I was the guy who had 'em round off. You can actually feel them getting round when they're going on."

Mark's third stop was the worst. It took more than a minute, and left Mark twenty-fifth. By lap seventy-four, when the next yellow flag flew, he had fought all the way back to third. This time, he came out in sixteenth. By the next caution period, he was ninth, directly behind Dallenbach. Dallenbach had not had a good experience with Roush Racing. He had already announced he was leaving at the end of the season. But he had always been friends with Mark. And he was a road racing specialist.

Before the race resumed, Dallenbach communicated directly with Mark on the radio: "Go to the outside. I'm going to bore a friggin' hole for you." By the middle of the next lap, Mark was third, trailing only Earnhardt and Petty.

With less than six laps to go, Petty spun and took Earnhardt with him.

Mark took the lead and finished 3.84 seconds ahead of Dallenbach. He must have passed a hundred cars in two hours of racing. "The door kind of swung open there at the end and we just slipped in," Mark said afterwards. "We were really fortunate to win this race." His first-place prize money was $166,110 - more than he'd ever won before. For Roush, it was his first one-two finish in NASCAR racing.

The following weekend, at Michigan, Mark won again. But it was with a different style. This time, he dominated, leading eighty-three of the last ninety-one laps to win by 1.28 seconds over Morgan Shepherd.

"I was more of a maniac this weekend, wanting to win two in a row," Mark said after the race. He had also won the Busch Grand National race at Michigan the previous day - his third Busch victory that year.

At Bristol two weeks later, Mark won the pole, but gave way in the race to Rusty Wallace on lap fifty, who led 410 of the 500 laps. But on a hot and sultry night, conditioning was key. Mark passed Wallace with only twelve laps to go and held off Wallace's desperate efforts to get back by.

Wallace, still feeling the effects of a terrible flip at Talladega in May, said, "I started getting a little tired there at the end. My neck started hurting real bad. I did all I could. He just got me. Everything

Right: Mark's third-place run at Talladega in July was without incident, but the race was marred by two big crashes that compounded the somber mood in the garage area in the wake of the deaths of Alan Kulwicki and Davey Allison.

from that darn Talladega wreck has hurt me because I haven't been exercising." Mark says, "I couldn't have done what I did if I didn't exercise five days a week,".

At Darlington the next weekend, Mark got off to a good start by winning the Busch Grand National race. Race day for the Southern 500 dawned gray and overcast, and rain delayed the start by three hours. Once it got underway, Mark led 178 of the 351 laps before it was called off due to darkness with just sixteen laps to go. He won by 1.46 seconds over Brett Bodine. It was the easiest victory yet.

As Mark pulled into victory lane, the setting sun peeked through the gray, rain-heavy clouds that had hung over the track all day. "I usually say a win is a win," Mark said. "But this is great. This is just a dream come true. Man, we're just on a roll."

With his victory, Mark became the sixth driver in the modern era of Winston Cup racing to win four in a row, joining Bill Elliott (1992), Harry Gant (1991), Dale Earnhardt (1987), Darrell Waltrip (1981) and Cale Yarborough (1976). And he headed to Richmond with a chance for five straight, unprecendented in the modern era, which began in 1972.

"Once you start winning, it's real addictive," he said after Darlington. "This is going to be hard to give up."

At Richmond, Mark won the Busch race, leading 185 of the 250 laps. He qualified tenth for the Winston Cup race, took the lead on lap ninety-seven and stayed in front all the way to lap 242.

But the longer the race went, the weaker Mark's car became. He began slipping back as Wallace took over on lap 267 and led the rest of the way. Mark finished fifth, losing fourth to Brett Bodine at the finish line.

The streak was over. But it had been the big racing story that August. And it helped take everyone's minds off the tragic month of July.

In winning Phoenix Mark displayed the close-to-the-wall driving style that impressed Larry Phillips in their ASA days. Mark's racing line was wider and faster than anyone else could run. He led all but one of the final ninety-six laps.

Right: Victory in the Southern 500 at Darlington made it four wins in a row. Mark spent the first half of the race swapping the lead between Dale Earnhardt and Rusty Wallace, then led all but three of the final 103 laps. NASCAR ended the rain-delayed race early because of darkness.

In the late afternoon at Richmond, Mark and Jack Roush talked about the car after the final Busch practice session. Their set-up was perfect and Mark won, leading 185 of the 250 laps.

The streak fulfilled Mark's ambition to win repeatedly in the Winston Cup series, but it had little impact on his efforts to win a championship.

Before the streak started, he was in fifth place, 455 points behind Earnhardt. When it was over, he was in third, but still 317 points behind. There would be

no catching Earnhardt in 1993. Mark finished the season third in points, 374 behind.

He did score one final victory in 1993 at Phoenix. He led 254 of the 312 laps and skirmished with Ernie Irvan at the end before beating him by a fraction of a second.

As the season ended, stock-car racing had become a game of aerodynamics and Mark had assumed more control than ever over how his cars were built and prepared.

During the 1991 season, car owner Robert Yates dropped the nose of his Ford and made the roof an inch higher. In effect, he raked the car, which raised the rear quarter panels and put them more directly in the air flow, thus improving downforce on the rear of the car. Allison had won five races that year. Mark had won once.

In 1992, Allison won five more times with his raked Ford, Mark and Roush had begun raking their cars, too.

Mark recalls, "Things were almost getting out of hand. Every week, somebody would come in with one jacked up even more. But now we've got a raked, downforce car that you can hold wide open a lot. It sticks to the race track. And the longer you ran, the more circles you ran around those Chevrolets."

Mark saw a way he could make his car even better. He asked his team for a raked car, but he wanted the roof brought back down an inch to the minimum height. That would still give his car superior downforce, but would make it even faster because the lower roof reduced drag.

His team did not agree. Mark recalls, "They said, "We can't get a motor in. And the tires will rub the front fenders because the nose will be so low it will be unbelievable. So we had a huge fight over this—a huge fight at our shop—and finally I got them to build me that car. We couldn't run a carburetor spacer because the hood was so close, so we had to give up about ten horsepower."

But the loss of ten horsepower was insignificant. "With that car, we won five of the last twelve races of the season," Mark says. "That's how important downforce is."

CHAPTER FOURTEEN

"I've got it all."

Above: Mark appreciates how his tough start in Winston Cup racing shaped his character. Family remains the most important thing in his life, the centering force that keeps racing in perspective. **Left:** Jubilant with his win at North Wilkesboro, Mark crowns himself the victor. The fall 1995 race was remarkable because it was the first time that every driver who started the event survived the 400 laps to take the checkered flag.

For NASCAR racers, the annual trek to Daytona in February represents a fresh start. But if the sport looked to the 1994 season as a way to rejuvenate from the tragedies of 1993, it was in for a rude awakening.

During the first hour of the first day of practice for the Daytona 500, Neil Bonnett was killed when he lost control of his car and crashed in turn four.

Three days later, Rodney Orr was killed in a savage single-car accident in turn two that tore the roof off his car. Two deaths in four days. Never in the history of NASCAR had two Winston Cup drivers been killed in such a short span of time. It was a somber Speedweeks.

In the Daytona 500, Mark was running third when he ran out of gas on the final lap and finished thirteenth. But he followed Daytona with four consecutive finishes in the top ten. At Darlington, Mark won the Busch Grand National race as well as the second round of the International Race of Champions, a series in which drivers from different racing disciplines com-

At the 1994 running of the TranSouth 400 at Darlington Raceway, Mark finished second, running himself ragged trying to keep up with winner Dale Earnhardt. "From lap one to lap 293, that was our guts hanging out every inch," Mark said afterwards. "He just blew us away."

plete in equally prepared cars. He finished second in the Winston Cup race.

Two weeks later at Bristol, however, Mark made the most embarrassing mistake of his career.

It was the last lap of the Goody's 250 Grand National race. Mark had dominated. The yellow flag was out. The race was destined to finish under caution. Three hundred yards shy of the finish line, Mark suddenly veered off the track and literally handed the race to a startled David Green, who was running second. Instead of winning his second Busch race of the year, Mark finished eleventh—the last car on the lead lap.

"What can I say? I thought the race was over. I made a mistake," Mark said. "That was the dumbest thing I've ever done in my life."

Everyone was so certain of victory, including car owner Jack Roush and crew chief Steve Hmiel, they let their guard down. They had their minds on the final Winston Cup practice soon to follow.

Roush had been spotting for Mark high above the track, "but I was on my way down the ladder," he said afterwards.

"I left the pits with five laps to go to work on the Winston Cup car," Hmiel said. "That's not losing, that's giving them away," Hmiel said. Green was so startled when Mark pulled off the track, he almost followed him. In the Winston Cup race, he was involved in a crash and finished twenty-first.

At Talladega, NASCAR's most dangerous track, Mark was running sixth when Greg Sacks got into Todd Bodine while trying to move out of the way of another car in the tri-oval. When Bodine lost control, Mark was snared in the melee and launched on the wildest ride of his career. His brake lines were cut in the initial impact and his car rocketed off the track at full speed, going straight ahead. His car ran parallel with the inside wall, then crashed head-first through the guard rail at the entrance of the speedway's road course. That hardly slowed him. He went through one chain link fence, then another, and finally slammed head-on into another guardrail near some fans.

Above: Thinking that the checkered flag had already waved, Mark pulled into the pits on the last lap while leading the Goody's 250 at Bristol, handing the win to a surprised David Green.

"I sure worried about things there for a minute," Mark said in the garage, nursing a variety of bruises. "It sure is a helpless feeling coming toward that guard rail with no brakes. It hurt bad. I know it wouldn't have slowed me down much, but I'd have sure felt a lot more normal if I'd been able to push on the brake pedal."

The entire ride was captured by an ESPN in-car camera mounted in Mark's car. "It hit harder than it showed on TV," Mark said.

At Watkins Glen in August, Mark finally broke through with his first 1994 win. Starting from the pole, Mark led seventy-five of the ninety laps and beat Ernie Irvan by 0.88 seconds.

"I was sure something would go wrong and spoil the day," Mark said after the race. "It kind of surprised me. But it was just hard to hold us back today. That's the strongest car we've had this year."

In the pits, Mark's team used a different tire-changing technique to adjust for the fact that in the Watkins Glen pits, the right side of the car is closest to the pit wall rather than the left. Reversing its usual procedure, the pit crew first

changed the right side tires, which were closest to the wall, then the left side tires.

"I think it did save time," said crew chief Steve Hmiel, "because the 28 car (Irvan) did it the normal way and we beat them just about every time. We worked on that for three days straight last week."

Six days after the Watkins Glen race, the sport was thrown into turmoil again. During a routine practice lap on a relaxed Saturday morning at the fast Michigan oval, Ernie Irvan suddenly crashed hard into the outside wall in turn two. The initial word from the crash scene was grim. Irvan might not make it.

Mark won again at Watkins Glen in 1994. By reversing the tire changing procedure—right side first rather than left—the team took advantage of the Glen's backwards pit layout. Mark had the hard-charging Ernie Irvan just 0.88 seconds behind him at the checkered flag.

For Mark, the shock was severe. He and Ernie had become friends in the previous months. "He's fighting to hang onto everything, I guess," Mark said, standing next to a stack of tires outside his team's transporter in the garage only a couple of hours after the accident. "This is just. . . . I can't find any words to explain it. It's just tragic. Ernie is just. . . . It just don't happen to your best friends that much."

Mark had a Grand National race in which to compete that afternoon. "It's harder for me to get in the mood," he said. "It's hard to sign autographs everywhere you step right now. It's a lot harder than it was this morning at eight." He finished third in the race and quickly left the garage.

The next day, in the Winston Cup race, Mark finished second. That night, he visited Irvan in the hospital for the first time. And later that week, he announced he would drive Irvan's Ford in the Grand National race at Bristol the coming week.

"I want to make sure this team can be an asset to the family and to keep it in good standing," he said at the time. "We're just going to keep on pulling for Ernie and hope we can get him back to 100 percent and back in these race cars at the race track. I sure do miss him. It doesn't seem like everything is complete without having Ernie there to race."

The next night, five days after the accident, Mark flew back to Michigan with Dale Earnhardt to visit Irvan.

"When I left, I felt I had been the one who had been helped," Mark said at Bristol two days later. "Dale and I went up together in his jet, and I was real glad Dale went, too. The doctor knew we were coming and already had him awake. I don't think he could see us because they had this stuff like Vaseline over his eyes to keep them from drying out.

"Dale walked up to him and said, 'Hey, this is Earnhardt,' and Ernie immediately got real excited and started waving his hand around, like he was searching for Dale's hand. Dale grabbed his hand and Ernie squeezed Dale's hand. Ernie was looking right at him, trying to focus his eyes on him. You could tell Ernie was real excited," Mark said.

"I went to his other side and I said, 'Ernie, it's Mark.' And he lifted his head up and his shoulders up. He was really moving around. He was reaching around for me. He was so excited, I wanted to calm

At the Busch race at Bristol following Irvan's accident, the No. 60 Winn-Dixie car sat idle as Mark drove Ernie's Ford in a show of support. Mark placed his name below the window, while Ernie's remained in the usual position on the roof.

him down. You didn't have to tell him twice who was there.

Through the fall, as Irvan slowly recovered, Mark was consistent enough to hang onto third place in Winston Cup points. But he couldn't win another race. His loss at Dover in September was a heartbreaker. He had led more than 150 laps and was half a straightaway ahead of Rusty Wallace with about fifteen laps to go when he bumped the lapped car of Ricky Rudd. The collision pushed a fender against a tire. The fender began rubbing. He was still leading with five laps to go when the tire blew. Mark slammed into the wall and finished nineteenth. Wallace won.

In the season's final race at Atlanta, Mark won again. It took him awhile to get to the front, but he led all but five of the last 100 laps and was 3.42 seconds ahead of Dale Earnhardt when he took the checkered flag. He shouted "We win! We win!" as he crossed the finish line, then thought he'd better double check.

"We're sure the race is over?" he asked on the radio. "I don't need to make another lap, do I? I just don't want to give it up."

Roush responded: "Take an extra one to make up for the one we missed at Bristol."

"We didn't turn it loose until really the second half of the race, and then I was just waiting for something to go wrong," Mark said afterwards. "It's so hard to win. And you never think you're going to win one of these things until you do it. So I thought I'd just take an extra lap just to make sure they weren't mistaken about how many laps we'd run."

It was Mark's fourteenth career victory. He also overtook Wallace to finish second in Winston Cup points, 444 points behind Earnhardt. He had won three more Grand National races in 1994, as

well as the two Winston Cup races. And at Michigan in the summer, before Irvan's accident, Mark had clinched the International Race of Champions title.

In 1995, Mark and his team had their characteristic slow start. It was spring before things began rolling. But in some ways, 1995 ended up being his finest year.

A blown tire sent Mark into the wall at Dover just five laps from certain victory. Mark was leading the race when he collided with the lapped car of Ricky Rudd and bent a fender against a tire, which ultimately caused the blow-out.

Mark's parents still attend races when they can. Julian, holding Matt, joined Mark and Arlene in victory lane following Mark's Busch win at Darlington on September 2, 1995.

In a season dominated by the new Chevrolet Monte Carlo, the Ford Thunderbirds as a group managed only eight victories. Mark won half of them.

His first came at Talladega on April 30. As he crossed the finish line, helped by the aerodynamic draft of having Jeff Gordon a couple of car lengths behind him, he told his team in a calm, even voice: "I can't believe it. Congratulations, boys. We got that big shove from the 24 car."

It was questionable whether any of the crew heard him. Their shouts on the radio were all but unintelligible as they deliriously danced on pit road. Finally, with his fifteenth career victory, Mark had won on a superspeedway.

A few laps from the end, Dale Earnhardt led Mark in a two-car breakaway. But Gordon was catching up with the help of Sterling Marlin, who had the fastest car, but had lost forty-three laps in the pits with engine trouble. Morgan Shepherd and Dick Trickle soon joined the Gordon-Marlin draft.

With two laps to go, Mark looked into his mirror and cursed on the radio. He didn't know if he could pass Earnhardt without drafting help, but he sure didn't like the looks of the oncoming juggernaut. Even before Earnhardt reached the white flag signaling the last lap, Mark decided to make his move. With that four-car freight train coming fast, he figured he might as well get in front of it. He went low to pass Earnhardt just as Gordon and the others arrived with a head of steam to push him forward.

"I couldn't believe Mark got by Earnhardt," Gordon said afterwards. "He must have had the momentum from me coming up behind him." Mark then blocked Gordon's attempts to pass. Behind

them, Shepherd drifted up into Earnhardt in turn two, spinning the champion, who crashed. Mark never saw any of that. He was looking straight ahead.

Mark's second victory in 1995 came at Watkins Glen after he took the lead from Wally Dallenbach with six laps to go. It was his third win in a row on the road course, and established him as the driver to beat there. His third victory came at North Wilkesboro in September. Every driver finished the race, with Mark leading the way by 0.88 seconds over Rusty Wallace. He led 126 of the 400 laps.

"We got lucky today," he said afterwards. We hit the set-up that worked all the time. Traffic can give you fits when your car is not handling, but my car was so good today, it wasn't a problem. If I really wanted to pass a guy, I'd just abuse the tires to get by. But with a lot of guys, I didn't even have to do that."

One week later, at Charlotte, Mark was in fifth place with about sixty laps to go. But Mark's car was best on long green-flag runs, and the yellow flag did not fly the rest of the way. Mark steadily moved up. On lap 297 of the 334-lap race, he went around Ricky Rudd and into second. He was still almost eight seconds behind leader Terry Labonte.

""I thought I'd done good when I got by Ricky," Mark said afterwards. "I couldn't even see the leader." That soon changed. With twenty-eight laps to go, Labonte's lead was down to 4.53 seconds. Labonte's car was drifting high in the turns. His tires were wearing out.

With twenty laps to go, Mark was about 3.5 seconds behind. With fifteen to go, Mark was 2.7 seconds back. With ten to go, he was only 1.18 seconds behind. A problem loomed ahead. His name was Jeff Gordon, Labonte's teammate. Gordon spent thirteen laps in the pits replacing a rear-end gear, but his No. 24 Chevrolet was fast. And he was hanging behind Labonte, apparently ready to block for him.

"Tell the 24 nice try, but we can't have that," he said. Hmiel assured him NASCAR was warning Gordon's team. With eight laps to go, Mark was one second back. The next lap, it was cut to 0.78 seconds. The next time around, he was eight car lengths behind Labonte and right behind Gordon. Mark got back on the radio and said simply, "Steve, the 24."

"Yeah, NASCAR is in their face right now telling them to get out of the way. It'll be fine," Hmiel replied.

Gordon moved out of the way to let Mark pass. Moments later, Mark moved up on Labonte's bumper. And on lap 331, he swept below Labonte on the backstretch and took the lead coming out of turn four. Earnhardt was not far back, and he soon got past Labonte, too. When the checkered flag fell, Mark was almost a second ahead of Earnhardt. He had only led five laps the entire race, but those included the final four. Hmiel exploded in rare exuberance on the radio.

"Now it's over! Now it's over!," he shouted. There was a pause, and then he told Mark: "Sorry I didn't talk to you much, Mark. I was afraid I'd mess you up."

"You did perfect, boy," Mark replied. "I was workin.' I didn't think I'd catch him."

It was Mark's second win in a row, his fourth of 1995 and the eighteenth of his career. Few have been sweeter. It was like those early triumphs while sitting high in the middle of that 1955 Chevrolet on the dust bowls of Arkansas and Missouri, when nobody expected him to win.

"Life doesn't get much better than this for me," Mark said in the press box. "It almost feels like it did in the old days. It's almost that much fun. I have traditionally been one of the least lucky guys I know. But things have gone well for us today, yesterday and another time or two this year, too."

Mark finished the season fourth in the Winston Cup championship battle, but what mattered most to him was that he finished the highest among all Ford drivers. Before the season started, NASCAR had approved modifications to the rear end of the Chevrolet Monte Carlo. Chevy teams were allowed to widen the back end of their cars by several inches, thus expanding the area where rear downforce is created, and making a better, more stable race car. It showed on the track. Chevys won the first seven races and romped to the manufacturer's championship.

But Mark had done the best he could. Under the circumstances, 1995 had the feel of a championship year. Mark had won twice as many races as any other Ford driver. And he had won, in a single year, on a superspeedway, a speedway, a short track, and a road course.

But then came 1996. Mark finished fourth in the Daytona 500, but fell out of the races at Rockingham and Richmond with mechanical problems and finished 37th, 21st and 34th in a three-race stretch in April. By then, he was fourteenth in points.

Mark passed Terry Labonte with four laps to go at the 1995 UAW-GM 500 at Charlotte. Jeff Gordon, thirteen laps down, appeared ready to block for his teammate. At the last instant, he moved over and let Mark continue his pursuit.

Ford Thunderbird drivers Rusty Wallace (2), Mark, and Dale Jarrett (88) run in formation during the Miller 400 at Michigan in June, 1996. Wallace won the race, Mark was seventh, and Jarrett was tenth.

But then he began climbing back up the ladder. The momentum didn't really get going until the summer. But starting with his ninth place finish at Talladega in July, Mark never finished worse than ninth for the rest of the year. He had fifteen straight top-ten finishes. But he couldn't find victory lane. He led the most laps at Michigan in August, but finished second to Dale Jarrett, who had the fastest car at the end. He won the poles at Bristol and Richmond (his third and fourth of 1996). He finished second at Charlotte and Phoenix. He won his second IROC championship. In the Busch series he had six wins, but for the first season since 1989, he didn't win in the Winston Cup series. As the season came to a close, Steve Hmiel became manager of all three of Roush's Winston Cup teams, while Mark's old ASA crew chief, Jimmy Fennig, became crew chief.

"We certainly put ourselves in position to win in 1996," Mark says. "But hopefully we'll be in the same position in the future and we'll get more than our share of wins to make up for those we didn't get in 1996."

The ups and downs have made him learn to appreciate what he's got, and how far he's come, and how his failure in his first attempt at Winston Cup racing shaped his character.

Mark says, "I'm glad it happened, because I wouldn't be who I am today had it not happened. I really like who I am today and what I have going for me. And I am not sure that I would trade that for, let's say, a 1984 Winston Cup championship."

As he talks, he is sitting in his motor home just outside turn one at Richmond International Raceway. It is a Friday night, the track is quiet, and he is without his family this weekend.

"I accept what happened the first time around because I've got it all," he says quietly. "I've got it all. I really do. I could win a few more races. That would be nice—if I could win a few more races. There's a lot of aggravation in my life, but it's still better than I ever thought it could be."

Following page: In the long shadows of the late afternoon, Mark and Matt find a quiet moment during a race weekend.

"Like, when you lose your license. And you go to the driver's license office and you take two IDs and you wait in that long line and you get up to the counter and the clerk says, "No, you've got to have three IDs. And then somebody says, 'Hey, it's Mark Martin.' And they take care of you."

"You can always have more, but I never dreamed it could be like this. I really have it all, from my crew chief, to my car owner, to my wife, to my son, to my father, to my mother. I've got it all."